Angels:
The Good, The Bad and the Ugly

By

Mark R. Erickson

authorHOUSE

1663 Liberty Drive, Suite 200
Bloomington, Indiana 47403
(800) 839-8640
www.authorhouse.com

First published by AuthorHouse 07/22/04

ISBN: 1-4140-0219-X (e)
ISBN: 1-4184-4301-8 (sc)
ISBN: 1-4184-4302-6 (dj)

Library of Congress Control Number: 2003098546

Printed in the United States of America
Bloomington, Indiana

This book is printed on acid-free paper.

Dedication

I dedicate this Bible study to USA Chaplain (Retired) and Pastor (Retired) Connie Walker. Very simply, he embodies the love, humility and faith that most of us can only look on in awe. God called him to be there for my family and me at a time when we really needed some spiritual uplifting. He was there for us in prayer, message and witness. He lives what he preaches. He preaches the Gospel. I thank him for encouraging me to continue with this Bible study.

TABLE OF CONTENTS

Lesson 1 – INTRODUCTION

This picture portrays an angel (Cherubim) protecting the entrance to the Garden of Eden after the expulsion of Adam and Eve. It is from the Dori Bible Illustrations by Gustave Dore and published by Belfoord, Clark and Company. (Some images © 2003-2004 www.clipart.com, item #83564)

The study of angels is a fascinating and exciting Bible study. It is an important study. This study will further help us appreciate how much God really loves His creation, humankind, and to what lengths He will go in order to save us. It is also important for us to study Satan and demons (fallen angels) to better understand our true enemy, and to bring us to closer dependence on Jesus as our Savior. Throughout this study keep in mind, we are not to seek angels. We only need to SEEK JESUS!!

The activity of angels will intrigue you, but a word of caution was brought from God by Gabriel: Do not seek angels. Seek Jesus! He is far greater than any angel! (ROLAND BUCK)[1]

Col 2:18 – Do not let anyone who delights in . . . the worship of angels disqualify you for the prize. (NIV)

Why study?

Why is so little prominence given it in the Confessions of the Church?

Because with the gift of the Holy Ghost at Pentecost and His abiding presence with the Church, the consciousness of the favor and nearness of God in Christ, completely subordinates their agency in the heart of the Christian. With the fuller appropriation of assurance of faith and of adoption as children of God, which entered with the study of St. Paul at the Reformation period, the chief allusions in the Confessions are in the cautions given against an abuse of the doctrine.

Is the doctrine, therefore unimportant?

By no means. But the Reformation had to protest against the excessive attention that had been previously accorded it. (JACOB)[2]

The acknowledgment of angels is needful in the church. Therefore godly preachers should teach them logically. First, they should show what angels are, namely, spiritual creatures without bodies. Second, what manner of spirits they are, namely, good spirits and not evil; and here evil spirits must also be spoken of, not created evil by God, but made so by their rebellion against God, and their consequent fall; this hatred began in Paradise, and will continue and remain against Christ and his church to the world's end. Third, they must speak touching their function, which as the epistle to the Hebrews 1:14 shows, is to present a mirror of humility to godly Christians, in that such pure and perfect creatures as the angels to minister unto us, poor and wretched people, in household and temporal policy, and religion. They are our true and trusty servants, performing offices and works that one poor miserable mendicant would be ashamed to do for another. In this sort ought we to teach with care, method, and attention, touching the sweet and loving angels. Whosoever speaks of them not in the order prescribed by logic, may speak of many irrelevant things, but little or nothing to edification. (LUTHER)[3]

God certainly doesn't want us to worship angels, but he does want us to be aware of them and their importance in our lives today. They are not just stories in the Bible, they are living, active beings working for God in the unfolding of his mighty eternal plan. (ROLAND BUCK)[4]

Opening Prayer

I give all praise and glory unto you LORD. May this Bible study on your precious servants, your holy angels, serve to build up and deepen our faith in you and your Word, and edify us more for your service.

Amen.

The Study

The structure of this study incorporates the elements of teaching and reinforcement, as I understand them. I tried to design a course requiring minimum preparation time for the teacher. I also pray that you will be able to place most of your time into prayer, spiritual development and material familiarization. I believe you will find this study spiritually filling and uplifting. In any case, you should finish this study with a deeper appreciation and understanding of God's love for us, as well as His creation, and His unlimited majesty. This study affected me in all these ways.

There are already a lot of books and commentaries on angels. But, I wanted to create something you could not find anywhere else. Therefore, this study uses only direct quotations from sources from diverse theological backgrounds. This is not just one commentator, but a collection of commentators. You may not agree with some, but you can still learn from them. You will also find that they do not agree with each other on occasion. We will never know it all, or agree on it all while we are still on this earth. I also recommend you take the time to read from the original works of these authors.

The underlying purpose for this Bible study, as for any Bible study, is to grow stronger and more confident in the Spirit and grow in our love for God. It is my prayer that this study will affect you that way. Remember; keep your focus on Jesus Christ. Nothing else really matters.

Copyright

I simply remind you that the sources used in this study are copyrighted and have given me permission to use them in the context of this study. Scripture excerpts are from the New International Version Bible as indicated. Most of these scriptures are quoted just enough to relay the pertinent content of the Scripture for the purpose of this study. I highly recommend you read the entire scriptures in the context of the Bible.

The Author

Like you, I am a student of God's Word, and have been an adult Bible/Sunday school teacher for many years. I researched this study for a class I taught in my congregation many years ago. I then reorganized it and added more material for another class just a few years ago. The members of this class and my pastor encouraged me to publish it.

Introduction

The following prayers by Martin Luther help set the stage for this study:

> Dear heavenly Father, I thank and praise you that although I am weak, and with the help of a hundred thousand like me I could not resist one devil, yet by the help of your holy angels I am able to oppose them all. And though I do not have so much as a tiny drop of wisdom, and the wicked and deceptive enemy has an ocean full yet he shall not know how or be able to harm me. My merciful God and Father of my Lord Jesus Christ, I owe thanks to you alone for this blessing. This is your glory that you so declare your honor, wisdom, and might in shame, foolishness, and weakness. As you enable us through your beloved angels to smite the devil, you alone shall have the honor of being a wise, mighty, and gracious God. Dear God, help us to do this. Amen. (LUTHER)[5]

> I give thanks, heavenly Father, through thy dear Son Jesus Christ, that Thou has protected me through the night from all harm and danger. I beseech Thee to keep me this day, too, from all sin and evil, that in all my

thoughts, words, and deeds I may please Thee. Into thy hand I commend my body and soul and all that is mine. Let thy holy angel have charge of me, that the wicked one may have no power over me. Amen. (LUTHER, Small Catechism)[6]

I give Thee thanks, heavenly Father, through thy dear Son Jesus Christ, that Thou has this day graciously protected me. I beseech Thee to forgive all my sin and the wrong which I have done. Graciously protect me during the coming night. Into thy hands I commend my body and soul and all that is mine. Let thy holy angels have charge of me, that the wicked one may have no power over me. (LUTHER, Small Catechism)[7]

Definition

The word whence we derive our word "angel" really means a messenger, not one who carries letters, but one who is sent to deliver a message by word of mouth. Thus, this name is commonly applied in Scripture to all messengers of God in heaven and on earth . . .. Therefore, all who proclaim His Word are God's angels and messengers. Thence is also derived the word "evangel," which means a good message. But the heavenly spirits in particular are called angels because they are the highest and noblest messengers of God. (LUTHER)[8]

The word angel means messenger, in both Greek and Arabic. They guard. They help. They heal. They save our lives or carry us away to blessed death. They send us notes or messages that we need; and always they are pointing to something greater than themselves. Always they say what angels say, "Don't be afraid. Don't worry. Everything will be all right. We are here." Then they send us the scent of roses or oranges as a sign, or give us a cup of coffee. And they never lay blame on us. They never say, "Boy, are you in a peck of trouble now." They never accuse, "You fool! Look what you've gone and done!" No, but always, "Don't be afraid. We're taking care of things. You're going to like this now." (BURNHAM)[9]

In our Judeo-Christian culture the word angel signifies their work as messenger, but other words for angels signify their essence. They are called gods, the sons of god, ministers, servants, watchers, and the holy ones. They constitute a court of heaven. They are called spirits, the heavenly army, hosts, cherubim, seraphim, living creatures. In the book of Job they are called "morning stars" and in Psalms "the chariots of God." (BURNHAM)[10]

Overview

Unfallen [*sic*] angels are given two specific titles in Scripture. They are called the elect angels (1 Tim. 5:21) which means they were elected not to fall and have been confirmed in their holiness . . .. What confirmed holiness means is that they are no longer capable of falling . . .. A second title unfallen [*sic*] angels have is the holy angels to contrast them with fallen angels who are wicked and unholy (Mark 8:38, Luke 9:26). (FRUCHTENBAUM)[11]

What do you mean by "heaven and earth"? By heaven and earth I mean all creatures visible and invisible.

Which are the foremost invisible creatures? The angels are the foremost invisible creatures.

How many kinds of angels are there? There are two kinds of angels, good and evil.

What does the Bible tell us about the good angels? The Bible tells us that the good angels—

A. Are holy spirits confirmed in their bliss.

B. Are of great number and great power.

C. Praise God, carry out His commands, and serve the Christians, especially the children.

What does the Bible tell us about the evil angels, or devils? The Bible tells us that the evil angels, or devils, —

A. Are spirits, who were created holy, but sinned and are forever rejected by God.

B. Are cunning, powerful, and of great number.

C. Are enemies of God and of man and endeavor to destroy the works of God. (LUTHER)[12]

Angels are mentioned in the Scriptures 273 times, in 33 of the 66 books, ... In the Old Testament, angels are mentioned 108 times in 18 books: . . .. In the New Testament angels are mentioned a total of 165 times in 15 books: . . .. In every gospel angels are referred to by Jesus Himself. (FRUCHTENBAUM)[13]

Make no mistake about it. Those invisible beings really do exist. Some are evil and work with Satan, and some are good and work with God. They are real, and they exist on both sides. (PITTMAN)[14]

I believe in angels because the Bible says there are angels and I believe the Bible to be the true Word of God. Christians must never fail to sense the operation of angelic glory. It forever eclipses the world of demonic powers, as the sun does the candle's light. (GRAHAM)[15]

What do angels do? They rescue, give aid, anoint us with calm and serenity. They deliver messages of warning or of hope. They guide us, teach us, answer our prayers, and lead us to death. But always they are at the service of God, and not themselves. (BURNHAM)[16]

Personal Account

Have you ever heard of someone that has personally witnessed a visitation of an angel? It seems this is one of those topics that the more you talk about it, the more stories you hear. There is one caution when listening to, reading or spreading angel stories. Satan can also appear as an angel of light. The mind can also play tricks on us, and is especially deceptive when it is a visual phenomenon. That does not mean all angel stories are bogus – just use caution. I have only used stories in this study from people I knew personally to be spiritual and trustworthy, or from other trustworthy, respected sources. The people I knew and whose stories I used did not rest their faith on an encounter with an angel. They were already people of faith. I trust that what they told me was true and accurate. I cannot speak for other stories I quoted, so you will have to use your own judgment. One pastor I know put it this way, "God gave us a brain, and we need to use it."

It is still about Jesus, not angels. Holy angels worship the same Lord we do. You will see this message several times throughout this Bible study.

As I was preparing for this study, a good friend related this story to me. Her husband owned a tree stump removal and trimming service. He was in business for himself. One day, he was in the top of a tall tree trimming out the dead branches when he lost his footing and fell. He fell through the thick brush of the numerous branches and came to the ground no harder than if he fell from a porch step. He was uninjured. His wife was on the job site with him and ran to his side. They both looked up into the tree in amazement. They could not discern any path possible to the ground where he would not hit at least a couple of heavy branches. It was as if an angel gently guided his way down and set him on the ground. You will not convince them that it was anything else. (Used by permission.)

Review of this lesson

Should we seek angels? NO, SEEK JESUS!!

Is the study of angels important? Yes. Why? They are God's creation. It is important to realize we have allies in the world against darkness. In addition it is important to know our enemy Satan.

What is the purpose of this study? This study will bring a greater appreciation of God's love for us.

What does the word angel literally mean? Angel literally means messenger.

Are angels real? Yes. There are holy and unholy angels.

Preview of the Bible Study

Lesson 2 – Who are holy angels?

Lesson 3 – What are the traits of holy angels?

Lesson 4 – How do holy angels interact with humans?

Lesson 5 – Functions of holy angels with humans

Lesson 6 – Organization of holy angels

Lesson 7 – Functions of holy angels with God

Lesson 8 – Who is Satan?

Lesson 9 – What about Satan's fall?

Lesson 10 – How does Satan interact with mankind?

Lesson 11 – Who are the fallen angels?

Lesson 12 – What are the activities of demons?

Lesson 13 – An angel of special status

Preview of the next lesson

The next lesson will deal specifically with who are the holy angels.

Lesson 2 - WHO ARE HOLY ANGELS

This is a view of the myriad of God's hosts as portrayed by Walter Russell, Bible and its Story Volume 5, published by Ira R. Hiller (Some images © 2003-2004 www. clipart.com, #300770)

Review of the last lesson
SEEK JESUS, not angels
The study of angels is important
Angel means messenger
Angels exist: holy and unholy

Preview of this lesson
Origins?
How many?
Natural appearance?
Age?
State of being?

Where did the Angels come from?
Scriptures
1. Gen 1:1-5 – God saw that the light was good, and he separated the light from the darkness. God called the light day, and the darkness he called night. And there was evening, and there was morning—the first day. (NIV)

2. Gen 2:1 – Thus the heavens and the earth were completed in all their vast array. (NIV)

3. Neh 9:6 – You alone are the LORD. You made the heavens, even the highest heavens, and all their starry host . . . . You give life to everything, and the multitudes of heaven worship you. (NIV)

4. Job 38:4-7 – . . . while the morning stars sang together and all the angels shouted for joy. (NIV)

5. Ps 148:1-6 – . . . praise him, all you shining stars. Praise him, you highest heavens . . . .. Let them praise the name of the LORD, for he commanded and they were created. He set them in place forever and ever; he gave a decree that will never pass away. (NIV)

6. Col 1:15-16 – . . . for by him all things were created: things in heaven and on earth, visible and invisible . . . all things were created by him and for him. (NIV)

Commentary
An angel is a spiritual creature created by God without a body, for the service of Christendom and of the church. (LUTHER)[17]

But the first three "days" of creation passed without benefit of sun . . ..
Not even our intellects can comprehend what is meant, yet we can have
no hesitation in believing the fact . . .. The only question is whether we can
find an appropriate meaning for the "morning" and "evening" of such a day
. . .. Note that Scripture never mentions the word "night" when speaking of
those days one after the other . . .. The knowledge of a created thing, seen
just as it is, is dimmer, so to speak, than when the thing is contemplated
in the wisdom of God . . .. Therefore, evening is a more suitable term than
night. However, as I said this evening twilight turns into morning as soon
as knowledge turns to the praise and love of it's Creator. Since my present
intention is to say something about the origin of the holy city, I must first
deal with the holy angels who form such a large and, indeed, the most
blessed part of that City, since they have never departed from it . . .. When
Scripture speaks of the creation of the world, it does not indicate clearly
whether or in what order, the angels were created. But, if they are alluded
to at all, it is perhaps under the name of the heavens . . . or more likely,
under the term light . . .. "In the beginning God created the heavens and
the earth," implies that before the creation of heaven and earth God had
made nothing. He began then, with heaven and earth. Now, the earth,
as Scripture adds, was at first invisible and formless and, since light was
not yet created, darkness covered the abyss . . .. Actually, the fact that
the angels are the work of God is not omitted in the account of creation,
yet it is not expressly mentioned. Elsewhere, however, Holy Scripture
bears luminous witness to the fact . . .. Thus the angels, illumined by
that Light which created them, became as light and were called "day."
(AUGUSTINE)[18]

In its epitome, v. 1, where we find, to our comfort, the first article of
our creed, that God the Father Almighty is the Maker of heaven and earth,
and as such we believe in him. The world is a great house, consisting of
upper and lower stories, the structure stately and magnificent, uniform
and convenient, and every room well and wisely furnished. It is the visible
part of the creation that Moses here designs to account for; therefore
he mentions not the creation of angels. But as the earth has not only its
surface adorned with grass and flowers, but also its bowels enriched with
metals and precious stones (which partake more of its solid nature and
more valuable, though the creation of them is not mentioned here), so
the heavens are not only beautified to our eye with glorious lamps which
garnish its outside, of whose creation we here read, but they are within
replenished with glorious beings, out of our sight, more celestial, and
more surpassing them in worth and excellency than the gold or sapphires
surpass the lilies of the field. In the visible world it is easy to observe,
Great variety, several sorts of beings vastly differing in their nature and
constitution from each other. Lord, how manifold are thy works, and all
good! (MATTHEW HENRY)[19]

The Bible states that angels, like men, were created by God. At one time no angels existed; indeed there was nothing but the Triune God: Father, Son and Holy Spirit. (GRAHAM)[20]

Angels have existed from the beginning of time. They were there before Adam and Eve walked out spellbound to explore their Garden . . . . After God created the angels, He created humans and told the angels to bow down to humankind, revere and care for them. (BURNHAM)[21]

How many angels are there?
Scriptures
7. Deut 33:2 – . . . myriads of holy ones . . . . (NIV)

8. 2 Kg 6:17 – . . . the hills full of horses and chariots of fire all around Elisha. (NIV)

9. Ps 68:17 – The chariots of God are tens of thousands and thousands of thousands . . . . (NIV)

10. Dan 7:10 – A river of fire was flowing, coming out from before him. Thousands upon thousands attended him; ten thousand times ten thousand stood before him. (NIV)

11. Heb 12:22 – You have come to thousands upon thousands of angels in joyful assembly . . . . (NIV)

12. Rev 5:11 – . . . heard the voice of many angels, numbering thousands upon thousands, and ten thousand times ten thousand . . . . (NIV)

Commentary
They are innumerable, myriads and myriads innumerable. Because of the concept of guardianship, there are always at least as many angels as there are human beings on the face of the earth. It could very well mean that there are as many angels as there are humans that will ever exist or that have existed, in combination or in totality. (FRUCHTENBAUM)[22]

The empire of angels is as vast as God's creation. (GRAHAM)[23]

There were countless angels everywhere. For a fleeting period of time I saw my own church building packed with angels. There were more heavenly beings than earthly beings! Hallelujah! (ROLAND BUCK)[24]

There is a whole host of invisible spirit beings working day and night, trying to influence the immortal spirit of man in his choice. (PITTMAN)[25]

An innumerable multitude! There are more angels in heaven than blades of grass in all the gardens in the whole world. So many men have never lived on earth as there are angels in heaven. (LUTHER)[26]

What do angels naturally look like?

Scripture:

13. Ps 104:4 – He makes winds his messengers, flames of fire his servants. (NIV)

14. Heb 1:14 – . . . ministering spirits sent to serve those who will inherit salvation. (NIV)

Commentary

. . . because angels are spirit beings and immaterial, they are generally not visible. But because they do have some kind of corporeality, it means they can appear in bodily form. (FRUCHTENBAUM)[27]

What are angels?
Pure and complete spirits, created by God . . ..
Why do we call them pure or complete spirits?
. . . in distinction from men who need bodies for the completion of their being. (JACOBS)[28]

How long do angels live?

Scriptures

15. Luke 20:35-36 – . . . and they can no longer die; for they are like the angels. (Matt 22:30, Mk 12:25) (NIV)

Commentary

First, all angels were created simultaneously . . .. Second, the number of angels do not increase . . .. Third, the number of angels do not decrease either. Angels, once created, exist forever. (FRUCHTENBAUM)[29]

The Bible seems to indicate that the angels do not age, and never says that one was sick. Except for those who fell with Lucifer, the ravages of sin that have brought destruction, sickness and chaos to our earth have not affected them. The holy angels will never die . . .. Because of this we can make a deduction: The number of angels remains constant. (GRAHAM)[30]

. . . invested with immortality like the angels . . .. (AUGUSTINE)[31]

In what state of being are angels?

Scriptures

16. Gen 1:31 - God saw all that he had made, and it was very good . . .. (NIV)

17. Ps 16:11 . . . the path of life . . . joy in your presence . . . eternal pleasures at your right hand. (NIV)

18. Matt 18:10 - . . . angels in heaven always see the face of my Father in heaven.

19. Luke 9:26 – . . . when he comes in his glory and in the glory of the Father and of the holy angels.

20. John 8:44 - . . . the devil . . . was a murderer from the beginning, not holding to the truth . . .. (NIV)

21. 2 Peter 2:4 - . . . God did not spare angels when they sinned, but sent them to hell . . .. (NIV)

22. Jude 6 . . . the angels who did not keep their positions of authority but abandoned their own home-these he has kept in darkness, bound with everlasting chains for judgment . . .. (NIV)

Commentary

The State of Grace is that in which they were all originally created equally wise and holy, and for eternal happiness (Gen 1:31; John 8:44).

The State of Glory is that in which the angels who abode in the wisdom and holiness in which they were created, have been admitted to the clear sight of God, and perpetually enjoy His goodness (Matt 18:10, Ps 16:11).

The State of Misery is the sad condition of the angels who of their own accord, and by the abuse of their free will, departed from God (2 Peter 2:4; Jude 6).

In the State of Grace they were able either to sin or not to sin.

In the State of Glory they are not able to sin.

In the State of Misery they cannot refrain from sinning. (JACOBS)[32]

They are holy beings and holiness in their case means that they are no longer capable of sinning because they have been confirmed in their holiness. Angels do not fall as they once did. (FRUCHTENBAUM)[33]

God is not called "Father" by the holy angels because, not having sinned, they need not be redeemed. And the fallen angels cannot call God "Father" because they cannot be redeemed. (GRAHAM)[34]

A good angel can no more turn into a devil than a bad one can return to the ranks of the angels who are good . . . angels have the certain assurance that their happiness is eternal. (AUGUSTINE)[35]

Personal Account

The Reverend John G. Paton, missionary in the New Hebrides Islands, ... Hostile natives surrounded his mission headquarters one night, intent on burning the Patons out and killing them. John Paton and his wife prayed all during that terror filled night that God would deliver them. When daylight came they were amazed to see that, unaccountably, the attacker had left. They thanked God for delivering them.

A year later, the chief of the tribe was converted to Jesus Christ, and Mr. Paton, remembering what had happened, asked the chief what had kept him and his men from burning down the house and killing them. The chief replied in surprise, "Who were all those men you had with you there?" The missionary answered, "There were no men there; just my wife and I." The chief argued that they had seen many men standing guard—hundreds of big men in shining garments with drawn swords in their hands. They seemed to circle the mission station so that the natives were afraid to attack. (GRAHAM)[36]

Review of this lesson

Where did angels come from? They were created. Why? They were created to Worship God, and serve us.

How many angels are there? There are more angels than we can count.

What do angels naturally look like? They look like spirits.

What is the life span of an angel? They are immortal.

Can they procreate? No.

Can holy angels still sin or fall? No. Why? The holy angels are confirmed in their holiness.

Preview of the next lesson

The next lesson will deal with traits of angels.

Mark R. Erickson

Lesson 3 - WHAT ARE THE TRAITS OF HOLY ANGELS?

Angels have many traits, one of which is great power. This picture depicts the destruction of the Assyrians by one angel as portrayed by Gustave Dore, in Dori Bible Illustrations, published by Belford, Clark and Company (Some images © 2003-2004 www.clipart.com, #83648)

Review of the previous lesson

Angels were created.

They are countless in number.

They are spirits.

They are immortal and cannot procreate.

They are confirmed holy and cannot fall.

Preview of this lesson

Intelligence?

Powerful?

Communicate with each other?

Sexual?

Emotions?

Lower than mankind?

How intelligent are angels?

Scriptures

1. 2 Sam 14:20 – My lord has wisdom like that of an angel of God—he knows everything that happens in the land. (NIV)

2. Matt 24:36 - No one knows about that day or hour, not even the angels in heaven . . .. (NIV) (Mark 13:32)

3. Eph 3:10 – . . . through the church, the manifold wisdom of God should be made known to the rulers and authorities in the heavenly realms . . .. (NIV)

4. 1 Pet 1:11-12 – Even angels long to look into these things. (NIV)

Commentary

Now, to God's good angels all this knowledge of merely material and temporal reality, which so inflates the demons, seems of little value. It is not that they lack such knowledge; it is because they love that Love of God which makes them holy . . .. Actually, their knowledge even of the world of time and change is greater than the demons because, in the Word of God, through whom the world was made, they contemplate the ultimate reasons why, in the cosmic order, some things can be used while others are refused, and nothing is confused. (AUGUSTINE)[37]

The holy angels gain a knowledge of God not by the spoken word, by the presence in their souls of that immutable Truth which is the only begotten Word of God . . .. They comprehend all this in such a way that it is better known to them than we are known to ourselves. . . . These angels were created and are something different from the One who created them. . . . the knowledge which they have in Him is as clear as daylight, whereas what they have in themselves is like the twilight. (AUGUSTINE)[38]

That the entire world is not a mass of flames, that all towns and villages are not lying in a heap of ruins, we owe to the working and doing of the good angels. They are far more sensible and wise than the evil angels, because they have a mirror into which they look, a mirror the devil does not have. It is called *facies Patris*, the face of our Lord God. This is why one good angel is far wiser than all the devils put together. (LUTHER)[39]

. . . to have wisdom means to have intellect. Because angels are by nature created beings, they have the limitations of creature hood. A created being is a creature and a creature can never have all the powers, attributes, and abilities of the Creator. Angels are not omniscient; they are not all knowing, but limited in knowledge. (FRUCHTENBAUM)[40]

Angels excel humankind in their knowledge . . .. And angels possess knowledge that men do not have. But however vast is their knowledge, we can be sure they are not omniscient. They do not know everything. They are not like God . . .. Angels probably know things about us that we do not know about ourselves. And because they are ministering spirits, they will always use this knowledge for our good and not for evil purposes. (GRAHAM)[41]

Do the angels possess physical strength?
Scriptures
5. 2 Kings 19:35 – That night the angel of the LORD went out and put to death a hundred and eighty-five thousand men in the Assyrian camp. (NIV)

6. Ps 103:20 – . . . you mighty ones who do his bidding, who obey his word. (NIV)

7. Dan 10:13 – But the prince of the Persian kingdom resisted me twenty-one days. Then Michael, one of the chief princes, came to help me . . .. (NIV)

8. Matt 28:2-4 – There was a violent earthquake, for an angel of the Lord came down from heaven and, going to the tomb, rolled back the stone . . .. (NIV)

9. 2 Thes 1:6-7 – . . . when the Lord Jesus is revealed from heaven in blazing fire with his powerful angels. (NIV)

10. 2 Pet 2:10-11 – . . . yet even angels, although they are stronger and more powerful, do not bring slanderous accusations against such beings in the presence of the Lord. (NIV)

11. Jude 9 – But even the archangel Michael . . . did not dare to bring a slanderous accusation against him, but said, "The Lord rebuke you!" (NIV)

Commentary

The destruction of Sennacherib's army of 185,000 men, in one night, by a single angel (2 Kings 19:35), is sufficient proof. (JACOBS)[42]

Angels enjoy far greater power than men, but they are not omnipotent or all powerful. In 2 Thessalonians 1:7 Paul refers to the "mighty angels of God." From the word translated "mighty" here we get the English word "dynamite." (GRAHAM)[43]

Angels are not omnipotent; they are not all-powerful and are limited in strength (Daniel 10:10-14, II Peter 2:11). For that reason Michael the archangel needed divine assistance (Jude 9). (FRUCHTENBAUM)[44]

Do angels communicate with each other?

Scriptures

12. 1 Cor13:1 – . . . speak in the tongues of men and of angels . . .. (NIV)

Commentary

When the escorting angels took me through that invisible dividing dimension wall that separates the physical and spiritual world, I carried with me my own personality. All the faculties that I had in the physical world, for example, memory and ability, were carried with me into the spiritual world. I was able to know all that I knew in the physical, only much more enhanced . . . We did not communicate there like we do here because, there, we communicated with our minds. It was somewhat like projecting thoughts by use of mind waves. We could travel at the speed of thought . . .. There was no sensation of movement at all . . .. I found that while I was in the spirit, I could not communicate with anyone in the flesh. I found that all spirit communication to flesh must be done through a physical body for clear communication. (PITTMAN)[45]

Angels have a celestial language and make music that is worthy of the God who made them. I believe in heaven we will be taught the language and music of the celestial world. (GRAHAM)[46]

Are angels sexual beings?

Scriptures

13. Gen 6:1-2 – . . . the sons of God saw that the daughters of men were beautiful, and they married any of them they chose. (NIV)

14. Luke 20:35-36 – . . . will neither marry nor be given in marriage, and they can no longer die; for they are like the angels . . . . (Matt 22: 30, Mk 12:25) (NIV)

Commentary

The Bible also teaches that angels are sexless . . . . This may indicate that angels enjoy relationships that are far more thrilling and exciting than sex. The joy of sex in this life may be only a foretaste of something that believers will enjoy in heaven, which is far beyond anything man has ever known. (GRAHAM)[47]

Another thing about the angelic body is that they do not reproduce after their kind (Mark 12: 25). Angels are always male and there is no such thing as female angels. But this does not mean that angels are sexless. Angels are always in the male gender and always appear as young men. The Greek does have a neuter but it does not use the neuter for angels; it always uses the masculine noun and the masculine pronoun. In the case of Genesis six where some fallen angels intermarried with human women, they were able to reproduce a grotesque race. But what they reproduced were not angels after their kind for angels do not reproduce after their kind; the angelic body is not reproducible. (FRUCHTENBAUM)[48]

Angels have existed from the beginning of time. They were there before Adam and Eve walked out spellbound to explore their Garden . . . . After God created the angels, He created humans and told the angels to bow down to humankind, revere and care for them. (BURNHAM)[49]

In the Bible the first angels were men. (BURNHAM)[50]

Do angels have feelings?

Scriptures

15. Job 38:7 – . . . all the angels shouted for joy. (NIV)

16. Lk 15:10 . . . there is rejoicing in the presence of the angels of God over one sinner who repents. (NIV)

17. 1 Pet 1:12 – Even angels long to look into these things. (NIV)

Commentary

They praise God, which is an exercise of the will . . . they worship God, which is also an exercise of the will . . . . Some angels chose to leave their proper habitation, which was an exercise of will. If they have joy, they have emotion. (FRUCHTENBAUM)[51]

When the local church assembles as a group of Christian believers, it represents in the human sphere the highest order of the love of God. No love could go deeper, rise higher, or extend farther than the amazing love that moved Him to give His only begotten Son. The angels are aware of that joy (Luke 15:10), and when a person accepts God's gift of eternal life through Jesus Christ, angels set all the bells of heaven to ringing with their rejoicing before the Lamb of God. (GRAHAM)[52]

What is their position in relation to man?

Scriptures

18. Acts 7:53 – . . . you who have received the law that was put into effect through angels . . .. (NIV)

19. 1 Cor.6:3 – . . . we will judge angels . . .. (NIV)

20. Gal 3:19-20 – The law was put into effect through angels by a mediator. (NIV)

21. Heb. 1:13,14 – To which of the angels did God ever say, "sit at my right hand until I make your enemies a footstool for your feet"? Are not all angels ministering spirits sent to serve those who will inherit salvation? (NIV)

22. Heb 2:1-2 – For if the message spoken by angels was binding, and every violation and disobedience received its just punishment . . .. (NIV)

23. Heb 2:5-9 – It is not to angels that he has subjected the world to come, about which we are speaking. (NIV)

Commentary

While they are far superior to what humans are, they are greatly inferior to what God is. (FRUCHTENBAUM)[53]

Angels belong to a uniquely different dimension of creation that we, limited to the natural order, can scarcely comprehend. In this angelic domain the limitations are different from those God has imposed on our natural order. He has given angels higher knowledge, power and mobility than we. (GRAHAM)[54]

However, God also foresaw that a community of saints would be called to supernatural adoption, would have their sins forgiven and be sanctified by the Holy Spirit, and finally be united with the holy angels in eternal peace, so that, at last, the enemy death will be destroyed. Men on earth, whatever the perfection of understanding they may reach, understand far less than the angels. (AUGUSTINE)[55]

The law is said to be received by the disposition of angels, because angels were employed in the solemnity of giving the law, in the thunderings and lightnings, and the sound of the trumpet. It is said to be ordained by angels (Gal 3:19). God is said to come with ten thousand of his saints to give the law (Deut 33:2), and it was a word spoken by angels (Heb 2: 2). This put an honour both upon the law and the Lawgiver, and should increase our veneration for both. But those that thus received the law yet kept it not, but by making the golden calf broke it immediately in a capital instance. They received the gospel now, by the disposition, not of angels, but of the Holy Ghost, not with the sound of a trumpet, but, which was more strange, in the gift of tongues, and yet they did not embrace it. They would not yield to the plainest demonstrations, any more than their fathers before them did, for they were resolved not to comply with God either in his law or in his gospel. (HENRY)[56]

Personal Account

A friend and member of my congregation related this event to me: "Shirly, my daughter, was on her way to take her son, Jason, to Day Care. As she came upon the railroad track (no safety guards as this was a remote area) her car came to a stop, and she couldn't cross the tracks. She pressed on the gas and checked the gearshift - - nothing could make the car go forward. At that moment she looked up, a train crossed in front of her. After the train passed the car was released from its 'hold'. She knew an angel had protected them— truly a miracle." (used by permission)

Review of this lesson

Are angels intelligent? Yes. They are much greater than humans, but they are limited. They are not omniscient, omnipresent, nor omnipotent.

Are angels powerful? Yes, much greater than humans, but they are not omnipotent.

How do angels communicate with each other? They have a spirit language.

Are angels sexual beings? No. There is no sex ascribed, but the male gender is used in the Bible.

Do angels have personalities? Yes. They have emotions, joy and will which are aspects of personality.

What is their position in relation to humans? They are higher for now.

Preview of the next lesson

The next lesson discusses how angels interact with humans.

Lesson 4 - HOW DO HOLY ANGELS INTERACT WITH HUMANS?

ABRAHAM WAITS ON THE ANGELS UNDER THE TREE.

Angels interact in many ways with humans. In this picture we see Abraham serving angels food as depicted from a 19th Century engraving in The Story of The Bible, published by Charles Foster Publications (Some images © 2003-2004 www.clipart. com, #580084)

Review of the previous lesson:

Angels have intelligence, but they are not omniscient.

They have enormous strength, but they are not omnipotent.

They have their own spirit language.

Angels are referred to only in the male gender in the Bible.

They have personalities.

They are higher than humans for a time.

Preview of this lesson

Visible?

Touch?

Communicate?

Eat?

Can we see angels?

Scriptures

1. Gen 19:1-2 – . . . two angels arrived at Sodom in the evening, and Lot was sitting in the gateway of the city. When he saw them, he got up to meet them and bowed down with his face to the ground. (NIV)

2. Gen 32:1-2 – Jacob also went on his way, and the angels of God met him. When Jacob saw them, he said, "This is the camp of God!" . . .. (NIV)

3. 1 Kgs 19:3-6 - All at once an angel touched him and said, Get up and eat. He looked around, and there by his head was a cake of bread baked over hot coals, and a jar of water. He ate and drank and then lay down again. (NIV)

4. Dan 10:5-16 – . . . there before me was a man dressed in linen, with a belt of the finest gold around his waist. His body was like chrysolite, his face like lightning, his eyes like flaming torches, his arms and legs like the gleam of burnished bronze . . . .. Daniel, was the only one who saw the vision; the men with me did not see it, but such terror overwhelmed them that they fled and hid themselves. So I was left alone, gazing at this great vision; I had no strength left, my face turned deathly pale and I was helpless . . . .. A hand touched me and set me trembling on my hands and knees . . . .. Then one who looked like a man touched my lips, and I opened my mouth and began to speak . . . .. Again the one who looked like a man touched me and gave me strength. (NIV)

5. Matt 1:20-21 – . . . an angel of the Lord appeared to him in a dream . . . .. (NIV)

6. Matt 2:13 – . . . an angel of the Lord appeared to Joseph in a dream. (NIV)

7. Matt 28:2-4 - His appearance was like lightning, and his clothes were white as snow. The guards were so afraid of him that they shook and became like dead men. (NIV)

8. Lk 1:11 – Then an angel of the Lord appeared to him, standing at the right side of the altar of incense. When Zechariah saw him, he was startled and was gripped with fear. (NIV)

9. Lk 2:8-9 – And there were shepherds living out in the fields nearby, keeping watch over their flocks at night. An angel of the Lord appeared to them, and the glory of the Lord shone around them, and they were terrified. (NIV)

10. Acts 12:7-9 – Suddenly an angel of the Lord appeared and a light shone in the cell . . . he had no idea that what the angel was doing was really happening; he thought he was seeing a vision. (NIV)

11. Heb 13:2 – Do not forget to entertain strangers . . . some people have entertained angels without knowing it. (NIV)

Commentary

The Bible indicates angels are more often invisible to human eyes. Whether visible or invisible, however, God causes His angels to go before us, to be with us, and to follow after us . . .. God is forever imaginative, colorful and glorious in what He designs. Some of the descriptions of angels, including the one of Lucifer in Ezekiel 28, indicate that they are exotic to the human eye and mind. Apparently angels have a beauty of variety that surpasses anything known to men. (GRAHAM)[57]

Angels always appeared as young men. It is not found anywhere in Scripture that angels appear in the form of women or children (such as cupids) or as old men. (FRUCHTENBAUM)[58]

These bodies are assumed temporarily, and cast aside when the purpose for which they have been used has been accomplished. They have no more identity with the personality of angels than the pen has with the writer, or the needle with the seamstress. (JACOBS)[59]

Angels can take on the appearance of a person, but their image is not necessary for their presence to be there. (BUCK)[60]

The good angels bring terror, that is, they come with a certain majesty . . . so that the people to whom they come are frightened. (LUTHER)[61]

They have the ability to take on a body, which has all the attributes of the physical flesh. When their assignment is over, they have the ability to put off that body . . .. The Bible even supports the notion that these angels, when in that physical body, also wear human apparel. (PITTMAN)[62]

Why do angels like disguise? They come as visions, voices, dreams, coincidences, and intuition, the whisper of knowledge at your ear. They come as animals or other people, or as a wash of peace in an ailing heart. Sometimes a stranger may come up and give you just the information or assistance you need. Sometimes you yourself are used as an angel, for a moment either knowingly or not, speaking words you did not know you knew.

But sometimes these beings come as angels in the very form that artists show—as beings of light, both with and without wings. Those who have seen them do not always agree on how they look. They are male or they are female, they are large or small; adults or children.

They stand, doing nothing, only looking in a puzzling way at the person who observes them; or else they weep (imagine!), or else they demonstrate a truth or bring a word of hope. And it is not to saints they come, but to ordinary people. (BURNHAM)[63]

In Scripture the visitation of an angel is always alarming: it has to begin by saying, "Fear not." The Victorian angel looks as if it were going to say, "There, there." (C. S. LEWIS)[64]

Can angels communicate with us?
Scriptures

12. Gen 19:12-13 – The two men said to Lot, "Do you have anyone else here—sons-in-law, sons or daughters, or anyone else in the city who belongs to you?" (NIV)

13. Dan 10:11- He said, "Daniel, you who are highly esteemed, consider carefully the words I am about to speak to you, and stand up, for I have now been sent to you." And when he said this to me, I stood up trembling. (NIV)

14. Zech 1:20-2:12 – . . . before me was a man with a measuring line in his hand! I asked, "Where are you going?" He answered me, "To measure Jerusalem, to find out how wide and how long it is." . . . And another angel came to meet him and said to him: "Run, tell that young man, "Jerusalem will be a city without walls because of the great number of men and livestock in it. And I myself will be a wall of fire around it," declares the LORD, `and I will be its glory within." (NIV)

15. Matt 2:13 – . . . an angel of the Lord appeared to Joseph in a dream. Get up, he said, take the child and his mother and escape to Egypt. Stay there until I tell you, for Herod is going to search for the child to kill him. (NIV)

16. Lk 1:11-20 – . . . the angel said to him: "Do not be afraid, Zechariah; your prayer has been heard. Your wife Elizabeth will bear you a son, and you are to give him the name John . . .. The angel answered, "I am Gabriel. I stand in the presence of God, and I have been sent to speak to you and to tell you this good news." (NIV)

17. Lk 1:26-35 – The angel went to her and said, "Greetings, you who are highly favored! The Lord is with you." . . . the angel said to her, "Do not be afraid, Mary, you have found favor with God. You will be with child and give birth to a son, and you are to give him the name Jesus. (NIV)

18. Lk 2:8-12 – . . . shepherds living out in the fields nearby . . . the angel said to them, "Do not be afraid. I bring you good news of great joy that will be for all the people. Today in the town of David a Savior has been born to you; he is Christ the Lord. This will be a sign to you: You will find a baby wrapped in cloths and lying in a manger." (NIV)

18. John 20:12-13 - Mary stood outside the tomb crying . . . saw two angels in white, seated where Jesus' body had been, one at the head and the other at the foot . . .. They asked her, "Woman, why are you crying?" (NIV)

20. Acts 1:10-11 – They were looking intently up into the sky as he was going, when suddenly two men dressed in white stood beside them. "Men of Galilee," they said, "why do you stand here looking into the sky? This same Jesus, who has been taken from you into heaven, will come back in the same way you have seen him go into heaven." (NIV)

21. Acts 8:26 – Now an angel of the Lord said to Philip, "Go south to the road—the desert road—that goes down from Jerusalem to Gaza." (NIV)

22. Acts 10:3 – Cornelius, a centurion . . . One day at about three in the afternoon he had a vision. He distinctly saw an angel of God, who came to him and said, "Cornelius!." . . . The angel answered, "Your prayers and gifts to the poor have come up as a memorial offering before God. Now send men to Joppa to bring back a man named Simon who is called Peter. He is staying with Simon the tanner, whose house is by the sea." (NIV)

23. Acts 27:21-26 – . . . Paul stood up before them and said: . . . Last night an angel of the God whose I am and whom I serve stood beside me and said, 'Do not be afraid, Paul. You must stand trial before Caesar; and God has graciously given you the lives of all who sail with you. (NIV)

Commentary

Not only does the spirit of man need a physical body through which to communicate to this physical world, but so do all the other spirit beings. The only way open for clear, concise communication from spirit beings to physical beings is through physical bodies. (PITTMAN)[65]

The shepherds did not see the angels. They saw only a great light and heard the word of the angel, just as one can hear it now or read it in a book, if eyes and ears are open to learn and rightly to use. But the Holy Spirit, who preached through the angels, caused the shepherds to believe. They were so strong in the faith that they were worthy to be spoken to by angels and to hear every angel in heaven singing a cantata just for them. (LUTHER)[66]

It seems that they take whatever form the visited person is willing to accept; and sometimes no form at all . . .. They don't seem far removed from natural events. This explains why angels are easily explained away, and why skeptics can pad down the corridors of their intellect, unhindered by the intrusion of the inexplicable . . . therefore it seems that angels bring messages in the form—even in the dialect—that each recipient can hear. (BURNHAM)[67]

Can angels take food?
Scriptures
24. Gen 18:5-8 – The LORD appeared to Abraham near the great trees of Mamre . . .. Let me get you something to eat, so you can be refreshed and then go on your way . . .. Very well, they answered, "do as you say" . . .. While they ate, he stood near them under a tree. (NIV)
25. Gen 19:3 – He prepared a meal for them, baking bread without yeast, and they ate. (NIV)

Commentary
Nothing in Scripture says that angels must eat to stay alive. But the Bible says that on certain occasion angels in human form did indeed eat . . . Not without reason some have concluded that Elijah indeed ate angels' food. (GRAHAM)[68]

During a visit one night, Gabriel said that God had sent me a little gift for my strength and energy as he handed me a round wafer approximately five inches in diameter and 5/8 inch thick, that looked like bread. He instructed me to eat it; so I did. It had the taste of honey. When I finished the bread, he gave me a silver-like ladle filled with what appeared to be water. I drank every drop of it, and an overwhelming desire to praise and worship God instantly came over me. Rivers of praise billowed up to God, bubbling up out of my innermost being, and for days after I drank this liquid, there was a sensation of "fizzing" inside of my veins. What an indescribably pleasant and exhilarating feeling it was! The effects were astounding because the first day after I ate the wafer and drank the water, I LOST FIVE POUNDS! The second day I LOST ANOTHER FIVE POUNDS! The third day ANOTHER FIVE POUNDS EACH DAY. Then it tapered off to about a pound a day. I had an excess of "flab," and that is all gone now. When I jogged prior to this, I quickly became winded, but now I have no breathe shortage at all. My strength and stamina have been fantastic! (BUCK)[69]

Personal Account:

A close acquaintance of mine related this story to me. "My father, when he was a small boy, was climbing on an upper story of a house that was being built. He walked to the end of a board that was not nailed at the other end, and it slowly began to tip. He knew that he was doomed, but inexplicably the board began to move the other way, as though a hand had pushed it down again. He always wondered if it was an angel's hand." (USED BY PERMISSION)

Review of this lesson:

Can we feel angels? They have ability to touch.

Can we see angels? Yes. We may see angels through dreams, visions, light, human form, and touch.

Can they communicate with us? Yes. They can talk to us, comfort us and warn us.

Do angels need to eat? There is no biblical indication they need to eat. Can they? Yes. And, they can provide food also.

Preview of the next lesson:

The next lesson deals with some of the functions of angels pertaining to humans.

Lesson 5 - FUNCTIONS OF HOLY ANGELS WITH HUMANS

One of the many functions Holy Angels have with humans is to escort us to Heaven as depicted in this picture published by Dover Publications in the New Testament – A Pictorial Archive (Some images © 2003-2004 www.clipart.com, #1035601)

Review of the previous lesson:

They can become visible to humans (dreams, visions, light, as humans, can touch).

They can communicate with humans (comfort and warn).

They can eat and provide food.

Preview of this lesson

Take care of us?

Serve us?

Be with us after death?

Watch us?

Revered by mankind?

Do angels take care of us?

Scriptures

1. Ps 34:7 - The angel of the Lord encamps around those who love him, and he delivers them. (NIV)

2. Ps 91:11-12 – . . . he will command his angels concerning you to guard you in all your ways; they will lift you up in their hands, so that you will not strike your foot against a stone. (NIV)

3. Dan 3:19-30 – Then Nebuchadnezzar . . . ordered the furnace heated seven times hotter than usual and commanded some of the strongest soldiers in his army to tie up Shadrach, Meshach and Abednego and throw them into the blazing furnace. So these men, wearing their robes, trousers, turbans and other clothes, were bound and thrown into the blazing furnace . . . the furnace so hot that the flames of the fire killed the soldiers . . . these three men, firmly tied, fell into the blazing furnace. Then King Nebuchadnezzar leaped to his feet in amazement and asked his advisers, "Weren't there three men that we tied up and threw into the fire? . . . He said, Look! I see four men walking around in the fire, unbound and unharmed, and the fourth looks like a son of the gods." . . . the fire had not harmed their bodies, nor was a hair of their heads singed; their robes were not scorched, and there was no smell of fire on them . . . . (NIV)

4. Dan 6:16-22 – . . . they brought Daniel and threw him into the lion's den . . . . A stone was brought and placed over the mouth of the den, and the king sealed it with his own signet ring and with the rings of his nobles, so that Daniel's situation might not be changed . . . . Daniel answered, ... "My God sent his angel, and he shut the mouths of the lions. They have not hurt me . . . ." (NIV)

5. Dan 12:1 - . . . Michael, the great prince who protects your people . . .. (NIV)

6. Matt 18:10 - See that you do not look down on one of these little ones. For I tell you that their angels in heaven always see the face of my Father in heaven. (NIV)

7. Acts 5:17-20 – They arrested the apostles and put them in the public jail. But during the night an angel of the Lord opened the doors of the jail and brought them out. (NIV)

8. Acts 12:6-15 - Peter was sleeping between two soldiers, bound with two chains, and sentries stood guard at the entrance. Suddenly an angel of the Lord appeared and a light shone in the cell. He struck Peter on the side and woke him up. "Quick, get up!" he said, and the chains fell off Peter's wrists. Then the angel said to him, "Put on your clothes and sandals." And Peter did so. "Wrap your cloak around you and follow me," the angel told him. Peter followed him out of the prison, but he had no idea that . . . he was seeing a vision. They passed the first and second guards and came to the Iron Gate leading to the city. It opened for them by itself, and they went through it. When they had walked the length of one street, suddenly the angel left him. (NIV)

9. II Cor 10:3-4 – The weapons we fight with are not the weapons of the world. On the contrary, they have divine power to demolish strongholds. (NIV)

Commentary

The angels are near to us, to those creatures whom by God's command they are to preserve, to the end we receive no hurt of the devil, though withal, they behold God's face, and stand before him. Therefore when the devil intends to hurt us, then the loving holy angels resist and drive him away; for the angels have long arms and although they stand before the face and in the present [sic] of God and his son Christ, yet they are hard by and about us in those affairs, which by God we are commanded to take in hand. The devil is also near and about us, incessantly tracking our steps, in order to deprive us of our lives, our saving health, and salvation. But the holy angels defend us from him, insomuch that he is not able to work us such mischief as willingly he would. (LUTHER)[70]

We Christians should have the sure knowledge that the princes of heaven are with us, not only one or two, but a large number of them . . .. And if we were without this custody, and God did not in this way check the fury of Satan, we could not live for one moment. A marvelous thing it is that the holy servants of God take care of eating, drinking, sleeping and waking children! It certainly seems to be an insignificant work. But the angels do it with joy; for it is well pleasing to God who has commanded them to do it. God created the good angels to serve and protect us against the wicked and harmful designs of the devil . . .. Therefore if the good angels were not present at the courts of the emperor, the kings, and the princes, the devil would not be slow to act but would start all manner of trouble so that the rulers would clash every hour. But at times our Lord God permits great lords to be at odds, lets the devil light a fire; but the good angels are present to extinguish the fire and to make peace. But when God withdraws His angels because of our sins or for some other reason, things are in a bad way. (LUTHER)[71]

As soon as one is saved, he has an angel assigned to him so that every believer has a guardian angel. Angels are often used to save or rescue believers from specific situations. (FRUCHTENBAUM)[72]

Has each child of God a guardian angel? It is going too far to derive such a doctrine from Matt 18:10 and Acts 12:15. The godly are frequently comforted with the assurance that they, are protected not by an angel, but by angels . . .. A number of angels— sometimes a host—attend one man, . . . and rejoice over the repentance of but one sinner. (JACOB)[73]

Were it not for the angel hosts empowered by God to resist the demons of Satan, who could ever hope to press through the battlements of the fiendish demons of darkness to the Lord of eternal liberty and salvation? The enemies of Christ who attack us incessantly would often be thwarted if we could grasp God's assurance that His mighty angels are always nearby, ready to help. Some believe strongly that each Christian may have his own guardian angel assigned to watch over him or her. This guardianship possibly begins in infancy, . . . (Matthew 18:10). The most important characteristic of angels is . . . that they work on our behalf. We should always be grateful for the goodness of God, who uses these wonderful friends called angels to protect us. Evidence from Scripture as well as personal experience confirms to us that individual guardian, guiding angels attend at least some of our ways and hover protectively over our lives. The Scriptures are full of dramatic evidences of the protective care of angels in their earthly service to the people of God. (GRAHAM)[74]

Then it dawned on me—guardian angels. I was looking at the saints' guardian angels. Each of these saints was accompanied by at least one guardian angel and some of the saints had a whole host of angels with them. (PITTMAN)[75]

Do angels serve us also?
Scriptures
10. Numbers 20:16 - He heard our cry . . . and sent an angel and brought us out of Egypt. (NIV)

11. Acts 12:8-11 . . . Then Peter came to himself and said, Now I know without a doubt that the Lord sent his angel and rescued me from Herod's clutches and from everything the Jewish people were anticipating. (NIV)

12. Heb 1:14 - Are not all angels ministering spirits sent to serve those who will inherit salvation? (NIV)

Commentary

I asked him [Gabriel] if they normally come in answer to a call for help. "No," he replied, "If the Spirit waited until you knew about an attack, you would already be in trouble! Chrioni said the angels had order to intervene, but not to interfere with what God was doing in man's normal course of life. (BUCK)[76]

They are our true and trusty servants, performing offices and works that one poor miserable mendicant would be ashamed to do for another. (LUTHER)[77]

Angels probably know things about us that we do not know about ourselves. And because they are ministering spirits, they will always use this knowledge for our good and not for evil purposes. If we, the sons of God, would only realize how close His ministering angels are, what calm assurance we could have in facing the cataclysms of life. While we do not place our faith directly in angels, we should place it in the God who rules the angels; then we can have peace. (GRAHAM)[78]

Will angels be with us after death?
Scriptures

13. Lk 16:19-22 - . . . the beggar died and the angels carried him to Abraham's side. (NIV)

14. Acts 7:54-55 – Stephen, full of the Holy Spirit, looked up to heaven and saw the glory of God, and Jesus standing at the right hand of God. Look, he said, I see heaven open and the Son of Man standing at the right hand of God. (NIV)

Commentary

Therefore, even when you come to die, you should say that Christ will be with you and will have an unnumbered multitude of holy angels with Him. You should know that angels are at your side not only in this life but also in death. At death I know not whither I am to go; but my guides, the holy angels, know it well. (LUTHER)[79]

As I gazed upon this beautiful place. I noticed a brilliant light within the tunnel. It was a bright, soft light, but was so bright that inside there were no shadows. I looked in amazement as I saw what appeared to be people walking in that tunnel. I asked my escorting angel, "What are these people?" He replied to me, "They are the saints going home." I discovered that demons were not permitted into the tunnel at all and that Satan had no power in that tunnel . . .. Although I was outside the tunnel, I could see plainly through the invisible shield . . .. As I was absorbing the facts, I began to be aware of other beings around the saints. These beings were all surrounded by a misty fog, but through the fog I could begin to make out shapes and forms. Then, it dawned on me— guardian angels. I was looking at the saints' guardian angels. Each of these saints was accompanied by at least one guardian angel and some of the saints had a whole host of angels with them. (PITTMAN)[80]

Even as the angels escorted Lazarus when he died, so we can assume that they escorted Stephen; and so they will escort us when by death we are summoned into the presence of Christ. The angelic emissaries of the Lord are often sent not only to catch away the redeemed of the Lord at death, but also to give hope and joy to those who remain, and to sustain them in their loss. (GRAHAM)[81]

Do angels watch us?
Scriptures
15. 1 Cor 4:9 - We have been made a spectacle to the whole universe, to angels as well as to men. (NIV)

16. 1 Cor 11:10 – . . . because of the angels, the woman ought to have a sign of authority on her head. (NIV)

17. Eph 3:10 – . . . the manifold wisdom of God should be made known to the rulers and authorities in the heavenly realms. (NIV)

18. 1 Tim 3:16 – He appeared . . . was seen by angels . . .. (NIV)

19. 1 Tim 5:21 - I charge you, in the sight of God and Christ Jesus and the elect angels, to keep these instructions. (NIV)

Commentary
Every true believer in Christ should be encouraged and strengthened! Angels are watching; they mark our path. They superintend the events of our lives and protect the interest of the Lord God, always working to promote His plans and to bring about His highest will for us. Angels are interested spectators and mark all we do . . .. (GRAHAM)[82]

They have the ministry of observation of believers to see how believers are acting and responding. (FRUCHTENBAUM)[83]

They [Prophets] are taught, also, by the angels of God who always behold the face of the Father and are commissioned to announce His will to others. (AUGUSTINE)[84]

Are angels to be revered?

Scriptures

20. Judges 13:15,16 – But if you prepare a burnt offering, offer it to the LORD. (Manoah did not realize that it was the angel of the LORD.) (NIV)

21. Rom 1:25 – They exchanged the truth of God for a lie, and worshipped and served created things rather than the Creator—who is forever praised. Amen. (NIV)

22. Col 2:18 – Do not let anyone who delights in false humility and the worship of angels disqualify you for the prize. (NIV)

23. Rev 19:10 – At this I fell at his feet to worship him. But he said to me, "Do not do it! I am a fellow servant with you and with your brothers who hold to the testimony of Jesus. Worship God! For the testimony of Jesus is the spirit of prophecy." (NIV)

Commentary

Although angels in heaven pray for us (as Christ himself also does), and although saints on earth, and perhaps also in heaven, do likewise, it does not follow that we should invoke angels and saints, pray to them, keep fasts and festivals for them, say Masses and offer sacrifices to them, establish churches, altars, and services for them, serve them in still other ways, regard them as helpers in time of need, and attribute all sorts of help to them, assigning to each of them a special function as the papists teach and practice. This is idolatry. Such honor belongs to God alone. (LUTHER, Smalcald Articles)[85]

We indeed should honor and revere them as God's ministers, and thank Him for what He affects for us through their agency; but this is far different from worshipping them or invoking their intercession. (JACOBS)[86]

Angels are never to be worshipped. They are so ordained and created that there is no place in their entire being for praise or honor. They are called the hosts of the Lord, and their purpose is to serve the eternal God. (BUCK)[87]

We are not to pray to angels. Nor are we to engage in "a voluntary humility and worshipping" of them. Only the Triune God is to be the object of our worship and our prayers. (GRAHAM)[88]

Even if we should wish to offer this homage to them, they are unwilling to receive it. And when, under a visible form, they are sent to men, they openly forbid it, as the examples in Scripture show. (AUGUSTINE)[89]

Personal account:

A close acquaintance of mine related this story to me. When my daughter was five years old and my son was seven, we were picnicking in the Colorado Mountains. They were playing by a small stream when we heard our son scream: we turned to see our daughter being sucked into the culvert. She had fallen on her head in the water. She was face down holding on to the sides when my husband grabbed her out. On the way home I was holding her and telling her how proud I was that she held on and how strong she was. Then I gave her a small lecture on danger—to never give up, and so on. She looked at me and said, "But Mommy, there was three tiny angels helping me; they told me to hold on, and I felt so strong." (USED BY PERMISSION)

Review of this lesson:

Do they take care of us? Yes. There is a possibility there may be a form of guardianship.

Do they serve us? Yes. They serve us in many ways we will never know.

Will they be with us after death? Yes. They will carry us to heaven.

Do they watch us? Yes. Why? They guide us, learn from us, and teach us.

Are they to be worshipped? No! We are not to worship or revere them— SEEK JESUS!

Preview of the next lesson:

The next lesson deals with the possible organization of angels.

Lesson 6 - ORGANIZATION OF HOLY ANGELS

Cherubim as portrayed in The Sacred Fire, published by Horace Liveright (Some images © 2003-2004 www.clipart.com, #100956), and Seraph and Wheels portrayed in the Bible and Its Story, Vol I, Published by Ira R. Hiller. (Some images © 2003-2004 www.clipart.com, #300770)

Review of the previous lesson

They guard and protect us, possibility of guardianship
They minister to our needs in many ways
They will escort us to heaven
They observe us and guide us, learn from us and teach us
THEY ARE NOT TO BE REVERED OR WORSHIPPED -
SEEK JESUS!

Preview of this lesson

Is there an organization or hierarchy?
What are Cherubim?
What are Seraphim?
What is an Archangel? Is Michael an Archangel? Is Gabriel?
How many?
Are there other angels? Are they also organized?

Is there an organization or hierarchy?
Note:

The order of presentation here does not imply that this is the hierarchy of heavenly beings. You will discover that great Christian thinkers will disagree more in this area of angelology than any other. That is probably because there is less concrete scriptural evidence to support a particular viewpoint. Read each commentary with an open heart and receive what God would give to you.

Scriptures
1. Dan 10:13 – . . . Michael, one of the chief princes . . . . (NIV)
2. Dan 12:1a - At that time Michael, the great prince who protects your people, will arise. (NIV)
3. Matt 26:53 – Do you think I cannot call on my Father, and he will at once put at my disposal more than twelve legions of angels? (NIV)
4. Lk 2:13 – Suddenly a great company of the heavenly host appeared with the angel, praising God and saying . . . . (NIV)
5. Eph 1:19b-21 – . . . when he raised him from the dead and seated him at his right hand in the heavenly realms . . . . (NIV)
6. Eph 3:10-11 – . . . the rulers and authorities in the heavenly realms . . . . (NIV)
7. Col 1:16 – . . . thrones or powers or rulers or authorities . . . . (NIV)

8. 1 Pet 3:21b-22 – . . . Jesus Christ, who has gone into heaven and is at God's right hand—with angels, authorities and powers in submission to him. (NIV)

Commentary

The angels are very well organized. The titles show categories of organization and degrees of organization. There are eight such titles.

First . . . thrones. Those angels who are on these thrones sit in the immediate presence of God (Colossians 1:16).

Second . . . dominions, which emphasizes the concept of rulership . . . rule in some specific area (Ephesians 1:21, Colossians 1:16). It includes higher angels ruling over lower angels.

Third . . . principalities. This emphasizes the concept of rulership in the category of governing . . . viewed as rulers of nations . . . (Ephesians 1:21, Colossians 1:16).

Fourth . . . authorities which means to exercise supremacy (Ephesians 1:21, 3:10, Colossians 1:16, I Peter 3:22).

Fifth . . . powers which emphasizes imperial responsibilities (Ephesians 1:21, 3:10, Colossians 1:16, I Peter 3:22).

Sixth . . . hosts which is the Hebrew word for "army." This title emphasizes their military organization.

Seventh . . . legions . . . emphasizes military organization. . . while the term hosts emphasizes the military organization as a whole, the legion is one division within the host comprising anywhere from 3,000 to 6,000 angels (Matthew 26:53).

Eighth . . . chief princes . . . an angel who heads up and rules over a nation (Daniel 10:13; 12:1). (FRUCHTENBAUM)[90]

He told me about different types of angels, such as praise angels, worship angels, ministering angels, and warring angels. Regardless of their function, their highest purpose is to exalt the name of Jesus! When that name sounds in heaven or here on earth, they fall face down and worship him because he is so exalted! Many angels have a rank or position in the heavenly army similar to a general or captain. (BUCK)[91]

Though some see the ranking of celestial powers as conjectural, it seems to follow this pattern: archangels, angels, seraphim, cherubim, principalities, authorities, powers, throngs, might and dominion (Colossians 1:16; Romans 8:38). Medieval theologians divided angelic beings into ten grades . . .. Perhaps any list that ranks angelic beings will err, but we can be sure they differ in power, some having authority others do not possess . . .. I think there are different ranks of angels and that the list given in Colossians does refer to these celestial personalities. (GRAHAM)[92]

Historical Concepts:

ST. AMBROSE (in Apologia Prophet David, 5) 1. Seraphim, 2. Cherubim, 3. Dominations, 4. Thrones, 5. Principalities, 6. Potentates (Power), 7. Virtues, 8. Archangels, 9. Angels

GREGORY THE GREAT (in Homilia) 1. Seraphim, 2. Cherubim, 3. Powers, 4. Dominions (Dominations), 5. Thrones, 6. Archangels, 7. Angels

PSEUDO-DIONYSIUS (in Celestial Hierarchy; also Thomas Aquinas in Summa Theologica) 1. Seraphim, 2. Cherubim, 3. Thrones, 4. Dominions, 5. Virtues, 6. Powers, 7. Principalities, 8. Archangels, 9. Angels

DANTE 1. Seraphim, 2. Cherubim, 3. Thrones, 4. Dominations, 5. Virtues, 6. Powers, 7. Archangels, 8. Principalities, 9. Angels (DAVIDSON)[93]

Note:
Only a few of the lists of hierarchies are given here as quoted by Davidson. Out of 13 different lists quoted by Davidson, Seraphim and Cherubim head the list in 10 of them. Archangels and angels are at the very bottom of six of the lists. Archangels and angels are near the bottom in two other lists and in one case (Dante) a level comes between archangels and angels. (DAVIDSON)[94]

Note:
This topic is fairly speculative and we do not need to get hung up on this. We just need to realize that God created a vast orderly organization of angelic beings to serve and worship Him and watch over us. Amen! SEEK JESUS! (Personal commentary)

What are Cherubim (Cherub)?

Scriptures

What is their Location?

9. Gen 3:24 - . . . on the east side of the Garden of Eden cherubim and a flaming sword flashing back and forth to guard the way to the tree of life. (NIV)

10. Heb 9:5 - Above the ark were the cherubim of the Glory, overshadowing the place of atonement . . . .. (NIV)

Description:

11. Ezek 1:4-28 - . . . saw a windstorm coming . . . an immense . . . cloud with flashing lightening . . . brilliant light . . . center of the fire looked like glowing metal . . . in the fire . . . four living creatures . . . their form was like that of a man . . . had four faces and four wings . . . legs were straight, their feet were like those of a calf and gleamed like burnished bronze . . . under their wings . . . hands of a man . . . had faces and wings and their wings touched . . . each of the four had the face of a man . . . lion . . . ox .

. . eagle . . . each had two wings . . . appearance like burning coals or like torches. Fire moved back and forth among the creatures . . . The creatures sped back and forth like flashes of lightening . . . a wheel on the ground beside the creature . . . sparkled like chrysolite . . . appeared to be made like an intersecting wheel . . . the wheels did not turn . . . . Their rims were high and awesome . . . full of eyes . . . . When the living creatures moved, the wheels beside them moved . . . the spirit of the living creatures was in the wheels. (NIV)

12. Ezek 10:9-22 - I saw beside the Cherubim four wheels . . . sparkled like chrysolite . . . they would go in any one of the four directions the cherubim faced . . . did not turn . . . Cherubim . . . Their entire bodies, including their backs, their hands, and their wings were completely full of eyes as were their four wheels . . . I heard the wheels being called "the whirling wheels" . . . . Each of the cherubim had four faces: cherub . . . man . . . lion . . . eagle . . . . Under their wings was . . . the hand of a man. Ezek 41: 17-19 - Each cherub had two faces. (NIV)

Ability to fly?

13. 2 Sam 22:11 – He [God] mounted the cherubim and flew . . . .. (NIV)

14. Ps 18:10 – He [God] mounted the cherubim and flew . . . . (NIV)

15. Ezek 1:24 - I heard the sound of their wings . . . . (NIV)

16. Ezek 10:5 - The sound of the wings of the cherubim could be heard as far away . . . like the voice of God Almighty. . . . (NIV)

What do they protect?

17. Gen 3:24 – . . . on the east side of the Garden of Eden cherubim and a flaming sword flashing back and forth to guard the way to the tree of life. (NIV)

18. Ex 25:17-22 - Make an atonement cover . . . . And make two cherubim out of hammered gold at the ends of the cover. Make one cherub on one end and the second cherub on the other; make the cherubim of one piece with the cover, at the two ends. The cherubim are to have their wings spread upward, overshadowing the cover with them. The cherubim are to face each other, looking toward the cover . . . . There, above the cover between the two cherubim that are over the ark of the Testimony, I will meet with you and give you all my commands for the Israelites. (NIV)

19. Ps 80:1-2a – O Shepherd of Israel, . . . you who sit enthroned between the cherubim, shine forth before Ephraim, Benjamin and Manasseh. (NIV)

20. Ps 99:1-2a – The LORD reigns let the nations tremble; he sits enthroned between the cherubim, let the earth shake. (NIV)

21. Isa 37:15-16 – Hezekiah prayed . . . "O LORD Almighty, God of Israel, enthroned between the cherubim . . . ." (NIV)

Commentary

. . . highest order of celestial beings are cherub or cherubim. The Hebrew word translated cherub has the root mending "to guard" or "to cover." It is used a total of 91 times. Twenty-seven of these times it is in the singular, 64 times it is in the plural. Of these 91 times, 90 of these times are in the Old Testament.

The Book that gives the most details concerning cherubs is the book of Ezekiel . . . .

First, their basic likeness is that of a man.

Secondly, each one had four different faces: man, lion, ox, and eagle. In this area they resemble the seraphim.

Thirdly, each had four wings: two on each side of the body.

Fourthly, their feet were absolutely straight.

Fifthly, the soles of their feet were like a calf's foot.

Sixthly, they sparkled like burnished brass.

Seventhly, they had the hands of a man under their wings on their four sides.

Eighthly, as to their appearance, they appeared in four ways: first, like burnished brass; secondly, like burning coals of fire; thirdly, like torches; and, fourthly, fire was in their midst.

Ninth, they travel with the speed of a flash of lightening.

Tenth, the noise of their wings was like many waters, like the voice of God, like the noise of a tremendous army.

Eleventh, they were connected or closely associated with the Shechinah Glory.

The last place cherubs are mentioned in the Old Testament is in Ezekiel 41:18-20, 25. This passage speaks of something future. From these passages seven major truths can be deducted about the cherubs:

First, there are three different types or categories of cherubs: first, those who have only one face and two wings; secondly, those who have two faces and two wings; and, thirdly, those who have four faces and four wings.

Secondly, they are closely related to the throne of God . . . .

Thirdly, they are very closely related to the Shechinah Glory.

Fourthly, the cherubim are closely related to God's presence.

Fifthly, they are concerned with justice and might.

Sixthly, they defend God's holy character and presence . . . .

Seventh, they have the ability to swiftly carry out God's will . . . . (FRUCHTENBAUM)[95]

Cherubim are real and they are powerful. But the cherubim in the Bible were often symbolic of heavenly things . . . . They had wings, feet and hands. Ezekiel 10 pictures the cherubim in detail as having not only wings and hands, but being "full of eyes," encompassed by "wheels within wheels."

While the seraphim and the cherubim belong to different orders and are surrounded by much mystery in Scripture, they share one thing. They constantly glorify God. We see the cherubim beside the throne of God.

The cherubim did more than guard the most holy place from those who had no right of access to God. They also assured the right of the high priest to enter the holy place with blood as the mediator with God on behalf of the people . . .. By right of redemption and in accordance with the position of believers, each true child of God now has direct access as a believer priest to the presence of God through Jesus. Cherubim will not refuse the humblest Christian access to the throne.

Many believe that the "living creatures" often mentioned in the book of revelation are cherubim. But as glorious as the angelic and heavenly beings are, they become dim beside the inexpressible glory resident in our heavenly Lamb, the Lord of glory, to whom all powers in heaven and on earth bow in holy worship and breathless adoration. (GRAHAM)[96]

Who are the Seraphim?
Scriptures
22. Isa 6:2-7 - . . . above Him [the Lord] . . . six wings . . . two . . . covered their faces . . . two . . . covered their feet . . . two . . . flying . . . calling to one another . . . holy, holy, holy is the Lord. . .. (NIV)

23. Rev 4:6-11 - . . . around the Throne . . . four living creatures . . . covered with eyes in front and back . . . lion . . . ox . . . man . . . flying eagle . . . each six wings . . . covered with eyes all around, even under the wings . . . never stop saying "Holy, Holy, Holy is the Lord God Almighty who was, and is, and is to come! . . . twenty-four elders fall down . . .. (NIV)

24. Rev 5:6-10, 14 - Lamb . . . slain . . . standing in center of the throne, encircled by the four living creatures and the elders . . . fell down before the Lamb . . . each one had a harp . . . holding golden bowls of incense . . . . sang a new song . . . the four living creatures said "Amen." (NIV)

25. Rev 6:1-8 - . . . one of the four living creatures said "come" (the four riders). (NIV)

26. Rev 7:11-12 - fell down on their faces . . . worshipped God. (NIV)

27. Rev 14:1-3 - . . .144,000 who had his name and his Father's name written on their foreheads . . . sang a new song . . . before the four living creatures . . .. (NIV)

28. Rev 15:7 - one of the four living creatures gave to the seven angels seven golden bowls filled with the wrath of God . . .. (NIV)

29. Rev 19:4-5 - The twenty-four elders and the four living creatures fell down and worshipped God. (NIV)

Commentary

From Isaiah 6:2-3, 6-7 four things can be learned about the seraphim.

First, they are around and surround the throne of God.

Secondly, they are characterized by having six wings. While angels have no wings, seraphim have six wings or three pairs of two. Each pair has a different purpose and function. The first pair of two is for the purpose of covering their feet; the second pair, for covering their face; the third pair, for flying.

Thirdly, they praise God to each other continuously. Without ending they say over and over again, Holy, holy, holy, is Jehovah of hosts; the whole earth is full of his glory.

Fourthly, it is a seraph that purifies the song of Isaiah.

From Revelation 4:6-11 seven things can be learned about the seraphim.

First they are round about God's throne.

Secondly, they are full of eyes in front and back symbolizing that they are able to see far beyond the human realm in order to be able to carry out God's providence.

Thirdly, seraphim have six wings.

Fourthly, the seraphim do not all look exactly the same. While all of them have six wings (the main common characteristic of a seraph), they do have different facial characteristics. There are four categories of seraphim based upon four different facial characteristics: lion-like, calf-like, man or human-like, and eagle-like.

Fifthly, they are full of eyes round about and within . . ..

Sixthly, they continuously praise God and say the same words recorded in Isaiah with a slight variation . . ..

Seventhly, whenever they say, holy, holy, holy this is a signal to the twenty-four elders that they too must now worship the One who sits upon the throne. The One sitting upon the throne in this context is God the Father. (FRUCHTENBAUM)[97]

Eight major truths can be deducted concerning the second order.

First, they are characterized by unceasing worship of God. They worship both God the Father and God the Son by unceasing worship.

Secondly, they are characterized by humility. This is visibly pictured by the fact that two wings are used to cover their feet and two are used to cover their face for they are standing in the very presence of God and surrounding the throne of God the Father.

Thirdly, they also have a ministry of purification of God's servants so they too can worship and serve the Lord. This is pictured in Isaiah six where the seraph purified the lips of Isaiah the prophet.

Fourthly, they lead in worship in heaven. When they say, holy, holy, holy, all the other inhabitants of heaven (such as the twenty-four elders) also begin to worship God.

Fifthly, their primary concern is to emphasize the holiness and worship of God.

Sixthly, they praise and proclaim the holiness of God. They do this each time in a three-fold way because they repeat the word holy three times . . .. That may very well be because of the trinity.

Seventhly, they proclaim that men need to be cleansed . . .. The means of cleansing is always by means of blood. Today it is the blood of the Messiah.

Eighth, the seraphim will be used for many of the tribulation judgments. (FRUCHTENBAUM)[98]

The seraphim and cherubim follow in order after the archangel and angels. These may possibly define the angelic authority to which Peter refers when he speaks of Jesus . . .. The word 'seraphim" may come from the Hebrew root meaning "love" (though some think the word means "burning ones" or "nobles").

The ministry of the seraphim is to praise the name and character of God in heaven. Their ministry relates directly to God and His heavenly throne, because they are positioned above the throne—unlike the cherubim, who are beside it. Students of the Bible have not always agreed on the duties of the seraphim, but we know one thing: they are constantly glorifying God. We also learn from Isaiah 6:7 that God can use them to cleanse and purify His servants.

They were indescribably beautiful . . .. The Scriptures do not, however support the common belief that all angels have wings. (GRAHAM)[99]

Two hundred years after Isaiah, the prophet Ezekiel saw not seraphim but the very thrones or Wheels of God. It is from his vision that the medieval scholars derived the class of angels known as wheels or thrones, the highest of the high. (BURNHAM)[100]

Who is Michael?
Scriptures
30. Dan 10:13b - . . . Michael, one of the chief princes . . .. (NIV)

31. Dan 12:1a – . . . Michael, the great prince who protects your people . . .. (NIV)

32. 1 Thes 4:16 - For the Lord himself will come down from heaven, with a loud command, with the voice of the archangel and with the trumpet call of God . . .. (NIV)

33. Jude 9 - . . . the archangel Michael . . . . (NIV)
34. Rev 12:7 - . . . Michael and his angels . . . . (NIV)

Commentary

The name Michael means "who is like God." Archangel means "the chief angel." This means that Michael is the one in authority over all other angels. He is not in authority over the seraphim and cherubim but he is in authority over the lowest order, the order of angels. The Concept of "archangel" is reflected in two other names Michael has. First in Daniel 10:13 he is called the first prince . . . . Secondly; in Daniel 12:1 he is called the great prince. There is only one great prince and that is the Archangel.

As the Archangel, his responsibility is to exercise rule and authority over the other angels. The responsibility of the good angels is to submit to the authority of Michael. Michael is also given the name chief prince. The term chief prince applies to angels who have authority over specific nations. As the chief prince Michael is responsible for the nation of Israel. That is why in Jude 9 it was Michael who protected the body of Moses . . . . Other things Michael will do in the future include the announcing of the rapture (I Thessalonians 4:16); in the middle of the tribulation Michael will cast Satan out of his present third abode in the atmospheric heavens to his fourth abode to the earth (Revelation 12:7-12). (FRUCHTENBAUM)[101]

The prefix "arch" suggests a chief, principal or great angel. Thus Michael is now the angel above all angels, recognized in rank to be the first prince of heaven. He is as it were, the Prime Minister in God's Administration of the universe, and is the "angel administrator" of God for judgment. He must stand alone, because the Bible never speaks of archangels, only the archangel. His name means, "Who is like unto the Lord."

In the Old Testament, Michael seems to be identified primarily with Israel as a nation. He is God's messenger of law and judgment. Bible students have speculated that Michael cast Lucifer and his fallen angels out of heaven, and that Michael enters into conflict with Satan and the evil angels today to destroy their power and to give to God's people the prospect of their ultimate victory.

Michael, the archangel, will shout as he accompanies Jesus at his Second Coming. (GRAHAM)[102]

Michael is the prince of the heavenly hosts, despite the fact that archangels rank second-to-last in the celestial hierarchy. Michael is the commander-in-chief of the celestial army. His name means "Looks Like God" or Who Is As God." (BURNHAM)[103]

Michael is head of all the great warring angels who do battle with the forces of darkness. (BUCK)[104]

Who is Gabriel?

Scriptures

35. Dan 8:16 - And I heard a man's voice from the Ulai calling, Gabriel, tell this man [Daniel] the meaning of the vision. (NIV)

36. Dan 9:20-23 - As soon as you [Daniel] began to pray, an answer was given which I [Gabriel] have come to tell you. (NIV)

37. Lk 1:19 - "I [Gabriel] have been sent to tell you [Zechariah] this good news." (NIV)

38. Lk 1:26-38 - "Do not be afraid Mary . . .." (NIV)

Commentary

The name Gabriel is Hebrew meaning "the mighty one of God."

His main work is to be a messenger of revelation; he reveals revelation from God to man.

Gabriel will also have work to do in the future. Luke 1:19 states that Gabriel is one of the angels that stand in the presence of God. In Revelation 8:2 there are seven such angels, which means Gabriel is one of the seven that stand at the very presence of God that will pour out the trumpet judgments of Revelation 8-9. (FRUCHTENBAUM)[105]

Gabriel is one of the most prominent angels mentioned in Scripture.

"Gabriel," in Hebrew, means "God's hero," "the mighty one," or "God is great." Scripture frequently refers to him as "the messenger of Jehovah" or "the Lord's messenger." However, contrary to popular opinion and to the poet John Milton, it never calls him an archangel.

Gabriel is primarily God's messenger of mercy and promise. He appears four times in the Bible, always bearing good news (Daniel 8: 16, 9:21; Luke 1:19,26). We may question whether he blows a silver trumpet, since this idea arises from folk music and finds only indirect support in Scripture. But the announcements of Gabriel in unfolding the plans, purposes and verdicts of God are of monumental importance. (GRAHAM)[106]

Gabriel is the chief ambassador to humanity. His name means "Hero of God." He is the Angel of revelation. He is majestic, richly attired and depicted in Christian iconography as kneeling before Mary, hands folded on his breast or carrying a scroll, scepter, or lily. It is Gabriel who brings good news. (BURNHAM)[107]

Gabriel is the leading angel, and he stands in the presence of God as a coordinator. God's organization is highly structured and is absolutely beautiful! (BUCK)[108]

Are there other archangels?

Note:

Material that would go in this section is purely speculative since scripture cannot support it. Five more names of archangels are listed in apocryphal writings as well as the names of numerous other angels, holy and fallen. Many lists of archangels and angels were accepted during various periods of the church before the Reformation. Davidson provides ten lists of seven archangels. The names Michael and Gabriel are included in each list. (DAVIDSON)[116] There also are many other names of angels given in other non-Christian sources. It is reasonable to assume that each angel as an individual also has an individual name. It is not the purpose of this study to delve any deeper into this non-scriptural speculation. Remember, SEEK JESUS!

Scriptures

39. Rev 5:11-12 – . . . heard the voice of many angels . . .. They encircled the throne and the living creatures and the elders. (NIV)

40. Rev 7:1-2 – . . . I saw four angels standing at the four corners of the earth, holding back the four winds of the earth to prevent any wind from blowing on the land or on the sea or on any tree. . . . another angel coming up from the east, having the seal of the living God. (NIV)

41. Rev 7:11-12 – All the angels were standing around the throne and around the elders and the four living creatures. They fell down on their faces before the throne and worshipped God, saying: Amen! Praise and glory and wisdom and thanks and honor and power and strength be to our God forever and ever. Amen! (NIV)

42. Rev 8:2-3 – . . . seven angels who stand before God . . . given seven trumpets. (NIV)

43. Rev 14:6-10 – . . . another angel flying in midair, and he had the eternal gospel to proclaim . . . to every nation, tribe, language and people. He said in a loud voice, Fear God and give him glory, because the hour of his judgment has come. . . . A second angel followed and said, Fallen! Fallen is Babylon the Great . . . A third angel followed them and said . . . .. If anyone worships the beast and his image and receives his mark on the forehead or on the hand, he, too, will drink of the wine of God's fury, which has been poured full strength into the cup of his wrath. He will be tormented with burning sulfur in the presence of the holy angels and of the Lamb. (NIV)

44. Rev 15:6 – Out of the temple came the seven angels with the seven plagues . . .. (NIV)

45. Rev 16:5-6 – . . . the angel in charge of the waters . . .. (NIV)

Commentary

Sometimes the term <u>angels</u> is used for all orders of celestial beings. All celestial beings are angelic beings. But most frequently the term angel applies to the lowest of the three orders.

The Bible also mentions other individual angels, which are not names but states what they do. For example there are seven angels standing before the presence of God (Revelation 8:2), one of who is Gabriel; it is not known who the other six are. Revelation 15-16 mentions seven other angels who will have the seven bowl judgments. Other angels referred to include the four angels of the four winds (Revelation 7:1-4), the angel of fire (Revelation 14:8), and the angel of the waters (Revelation 16:5). (FRUCHTENBAUM)[109]

Personal account:

The year was 1938 . . . I was standing under the shed of a warehouse loading dock waiting for the freight train that was in the yards taking on water and coal to start moving out. I stood waiting until I saw a boxcar with a door open, then I started running to jump in. The boxcar was rather high off the ground because of the terrain. When I jumped, I only got halfway in . . .. I couldn't pull myself in because I had nothing to hold onto. The train was gaining speed very fast as I lay there trying to pull myself in, my arms outstretched on the floor. I knew if I fell it would be certain death under the wheels of that freight train. I will never forget that moment. I thought my time had come. As I was struggling on the floor, I can recall saying, "O God, please don't let me die here." I raised my head enough to see a very large black man, in his thirties standing they're looking at me. He didn't say anything to me and I didn't say anything to him. He reached down, got hold of me by the arms, and pulled me into the boxcar. I lay on the floor face down for about half a minute to catch my breath and regain my strength. When I got up to thank the man, he was nowhere to be seen. The boxcar was completely empty; the other door was closed, and the train was moving too fast for anyone to jump out and live. There was no one in that boxcar but me. The black man had vanished. (BURNHAM)[110]

Review of this lesson

Is there a hierarchy? There is an organization or hierarchy of heavenly beings.

What are Cherubim? They may be the highest order of heavenly beings. They guard God's throne and praise Him.

What are Seraphim? Maybe they are the second highest order of heavenly beings. They lead praise and worship of God.

What is an Archangel? Archangel means chief angel. Some commentaries place them as the highest order of angels. The term is only used with Michael in the Bible.

Who is Michael? Michael is an Archangel. He is possibly the chief archangel and/or the angel over Israel.

Who Is Gabriel? Gabriel is God's chief messenger of prophecy, revelation, and good news. He is not specifically mentioned in scripture as being an archangel.

How many archangels are there? The Bible specifically names only one archangel. - Michael.

Are there other angels? There are many other angels. Are they also organized? Yes.

Preview of the next lesson:

The next lesson deals with some of the functions of angels pertaining to God.

Lesson 7 - FUNCTIONS OF HOLY ANGELS WITH GOD

Choirs of angels in heaven as portrayed in Dante's The Vision (The Divine Comedy) by G. Fattorusso (Some images © 2003-2004 www.clipart.com, #667993).

Review of the previous lesson

There is a hierarchy of heavenly beings.

Cherubim may be the highest order of heavenly beings. They guard God's throne and praise God.

Seraphim are a high order of heavenly beings. They lead praise and worship God.

Only one archangel is named in the Bible. He is the chief angel. Michael is the archangel. Gabriel is not named as an archangel in the Bible. The Bible specifically names only one archangel.

There are other angels. They are also organized.

Preview of this lesson

Relation to God?
Relation to Christ?
Relation to Holy Spirit?
Come in wrath?

What are functions in relation to God?

Scriptures

1. Ps 103:20-21 – Praise the LORD, you his angels, you mighty ones who do his bidding, who obey his word. Praise the LORD, all his heavenly hosts, you his servants who do his will. (NIV)

2. Lk 2:13-15 – Suddenly a great company of the heavenly host appeared with the angel, praising God and saying, "Glory to God in the highest, and on earth peace to men on whom his favor rests." (NIV)

3. Rev 7:11-12 – All the angels were standing around the throne and around the elders and the four living creatures. They fell down on their faces before the throne and worshipped God, saying: Amen! Praise and glory and wisdom and thanks and honor and power and strength be to our God forever and ever. Amen! (NIV)

Commentary

He does many things by the ministry of angels, but their only source of beatitude is God Himself. And he Himself, and not the angels, is the source of men's beatitude, even though He sometimes uses angels as messengers to men.

Holy angels gain knowledge of God not by the spoken word but by the presence in their souls of that immutable Truth which is the only begotten

Word of God . . .. They comprehend all this in such a way that it is better known to them than we are known to ourselves. (AUGUSTINE)[111]

God is not called Father by the holy angels because, not having sinned, they need not be redeemed. And the fallen angels cannot call God Father because they cannot be redeemed.

But angels do not spend all their time in heaven. They are not omnipresent . . .. But when angels do stand before the throne of God, indeed they worship and adore their creator. (GRAHAM)[112]

At the throne of God, the angels have no form at all, but come as pure, raw energy, great sweeping balls of fire, like supernovas, circling, whirling, wheeling in black space. They are called Wheels or Thrones and they cannot even be depicted except symbolically . . .. (BURNHAM)[113]

There are four specific ministries:
Firstly . . . employed in the worship of God and they actively worship God . . ..
Secondly . . . they execute God's will . . ..
Thirdly . . . angels rejoice in the work of God . . ..
Fourthly, they execute God's judgments. (FRUCHTENBAUM)[114]

The angels said, "We want you to join in worship with us," and Pastor Buck was immediately given a language he had never spoken before. For thirty-five minutes, Gabriel, Chrioni, Cyprion, and Pastor Buck praised and worshipped God together. He said praise flowed through him like a "river language" which he couldn't start or stop himself! As they were all worshipping and praising God together, Pastor Buck opened his eyes and saw something he could hardly comprehend. Then he looked at Cyprion's feet, and they were about eighteen inches off the floor, then he looked at his own feet, and to his utter amazement they were also about eighteen inches off the floor! Gabriel . . . said that from the highest to the lowest of angels, to human beings, when we praise and worship God, we are all on the same level . . . worship is the best equalizer there is between heaven and earth. (BUCK)[115]

What are functions in relation to Christ?
Scriptures
4. Ps 91:12 – . . . he will command his angels concerning you to guard you in all your ways; they will lift you up in their hands, so that you will not strike your foot against a stone. (NIV)
5. Matt 24:30-31 - . . . the sign of the Son of Man will appear in the sky . . .. And he will send his angels with a loud trumpet call . . .. (NIV)

6. Matt 25:31 - When the Son of Man comes in his glory, and all the angels with him, he will sit on his throne in heavenly glory. (NIV)

7. Matt 26:53-53 – Do you think I cannot call on my Father, and he will at once put at my disposal more than twelve legions of angels? (NIV)

8. Lk 22:41-44 – He . . . prayed, "Father, if you are willing, take this cup from me; yet not my will, but yours be done. "An angel from heaven appeared to him and strengthened him. (NIV)

9. Jn 1:51 – ". . . you shall see heaven open, and the angels of God ascending and descending on the Son of Man." (NIV)

10. 2 Thes 1:6-7 - . . . when the Lord Jesus is revealed from heaven in blazing fire with his powerful angels.

11. Heb 1:6 - . . . when God brings his firstborn into the world, he says, Let all God's angels worship him. (NIV)

12. Rev 5:11,12 – . . . the voice of many angels . . .. In a loud voice they sang: "Worthy is the Lamb, who was slain, to receive power and wealth and wisdom and strength and honor and glory and praise!" (NIV)

Commentary

They are motivated by an inexhaustible love for God and are jealous to see that the will of God in Jesus Christ is fulfilled in us.

It would take an entire book to spell out in detail how the life of Jesus was intertwined with the attending ministry of angels. Before He was here they followed His orders. And since He ascended into heaven they have worshipped Him before the throne of God as the Lamb slain for our salvation. (GRAHAM)[116]

Angels were used in five specific periods of the life of Christ.

His birth . . . predicted the birth . . . announced the birth . . . warned Joseph to flee Bethlehem . . . told Joseph to leave Egypt and return to Israel.

Ministry of Jesus . . . predicted . . . used to minister to Him in His temptations . . . throughout His ministry angels were ascending and descending upon the Son of Man . . . twelve legions of angels ready to defend Him at His trial if He needed them.

The resurrection . . . rolled the stone away . . . used to announce the resurrection.

The ascension . . . Angels announced that this same Jesus now departing will come again.

Future . . . Angels will come with Him in the clouds of heaven at the Second Coming. (FRUCHTENBAUM)[117]

What are functions with the Holy Spirit?

Note:

This section has no scripture to support it so be led by your heart.

Commentary

Moreover, we should not confuse angels, whether visible or invisible, with the Holy Spirit, the third person of the Trinity and Himself, God. Angels do not indwell men; the Holy Spirit seals them and indwells them when He has regenerated them.

Nothing in the Bible indicates that the Holy Spirit indwells angels as he does redeem people. Since He seals believers when they accept Christ, such sealing would be unnecessary for the angels who never fell and who therefore need no salvation. (GRAHAM)[118]

Theologically, I knew that the Holy Spirit was everywhere at once, but it took on new meaning when he [Gabriel] told me that the Holy Spirit constantly monitors the whole earth and picks up the signals from everywhere at once. He even hears the softest footsteps, and he cares! Gabriel said since the Holy Spirit monitors everything on earth, he will not allow him [Satan] to do this. When he sees the activity of Satan becoming dangerous, he dispatches hosts of angels to straighten out the situation. (BUCK)[119]

Do angels come in wrath?

Scriptures

13. 1 Chr 21:15 – . . . God sent an angel to destroy Jerusalem . . .. (NIV)

14. 2 Chr 32:21 - . . . the LORD sent an angel, who annihilated all the fighting men and the leaders and officers in the camp of the Assyrian king . . .. (NIV)

15. Matt 13:41-43 - The Son of Man will send out his angels, and they will weed out of his kingdom everything that causes sin and all who do evil. They will throw them into the fiery furnace, where there will be weeping and gnashing of teeth. (NIV)

16. Matt 25:31-33 - When the Son of Man comes in his glory, and all the angels with him . . . he will separate the people one from another as a shepherd separates the sheep from the goats. (NIV)

17. Mk 13:26,27 - . . . he will send his angels and gather his elect from the four winds, from the ends of the earth to the ends of the heavens. (NIV)

18. Acts 12:21-23 – . . . because Herod did not give praise to God, an angel of the Lord struck him down . . .. (NIV)

19. 1 Cor 10:10 - And do not grumble as some of them did— and were killed by the destroying angel. (NIV)

20. Rev 6:1-8 – . . . Lamb opened the first of the seven seals . . . a white horse! Its rider held a bow, and he was given a crown, and he rode out as a conqueror . . . the second seal . . .another horse came out, a fiery red one. Its rider was given power to take peace from the earth and to

make men slay each other . . .the third seal . . . a black horse! Its rider was holding a pair of scales in his hand . . . the fourth seal . . . a pale horse! Its rider was named Death, and Hades was following close behind him. They were given power over a fourth of the earth to kill by sword, famine and plague, and by the wild beasts of the earth. (NIV)

21. Rev 7:1-2 – . . . I saw four angels standing at the four corners of the earth, holding back the four winds of the earth to prevent any wind from blowing on the land or on the sea or on any tree. Then I saw another angel coming up from the east, having the seal of the living God. He called out in a loud voice to the four angels who had been given power to harm the land and the sea. (NIV)

22. Rev 8:6-10:11 - . . . the seven angels who had the seven trumpets prepared to sound them . . . first angel . . . hail and fire mixed with blood . . . third of the earth burned up . . . second angel . . . huge mountain all ablaze, thrown into the sea . . . third of the living creatures died . . . third of ships were destroyed . . . third angel . . . great star, blazing . . .. Wormwood . . .. A third of the rivers . . . springs . . . turned bitter . . . many people died . . . fourth angel . . . third . . . sun . . . moon . . . stars . . . turned dark . . . fifth angel . . . star fell . . . given key to Abyss . . . sun and sky were darkened by the smoke . . . locusts came like that of scorpions . . . the first woe . . . sixth angel . . . release the four angels who were bound . . . to kill a third of mankind . . . another mighty angel . . . robed in a cloud; his face was like the sun and his legs were like fiery pillars . . . holding a scroll . . . his right foot on the sea and his left foot on the land . . . a voice from heaven . . . seal up what the seven thunder have said and do not write it down. (NIV)

23. Rev 14:14-20 - . . . another angel . . .. Take your sickle . . .. Another angel . . . he too had a sharp sickle . . . gather the clusters of grapes . . .. They were trampled in the winepress of God's wrath. (NIV)

24. Rev 15:6-16:21 - . . . gave to the seven angels seven golden bowls filled with the wrath of God . . . first angel . . . painful sores . . . second angel . . . the sea . . . turned into blood . . . every living thing in the sea died . . . third angel . . . rivers and springs . . . became blood . . . fourth angel . . . the sun . . . scorch the people with fire . . . fifth angel . . . throne of the beast . . . kingdom plunged into darkness . . .. Men gnawed their tongues in agony . . . sixth angel . . . great river Euphrates . . . dried up to prepare the way for the kings from the East . . . seventh angel . . . air . . . lightening, rumblings, peals of thunder, and a severe earthquake . . . the great city split into three parts, cities of the nations collapsed . . .. Every island fled away and the mountains could not be found. From the sky huge hail stones of about a hundred pounds each fell on men. (NIV)

Commentary

For the holy angels punish without anger those whom the eternal law of God has delivered to them for punishment, succor the suffering without suffering compassion, and rescue from peril those whom they love without sharing their fear. (AUGUSTINE)[120]

The Bible says that throughout history angels have worked to carry out God's judgments, directing the destinies of nations disobedient to God . . . . Further, at the "end of the age" angels will execute judgment on those who have rejected God's love. (GRAHAM)[121]

Personal account:

Another story from a long time close Christian friend.

I was driving down a major North Dakota highway late one night. Suddenly, I heard an audible voice. Since I had thought I was alone in the car, initially, I was quite frightened. I thought that perhaps someone had broken into my car while it was parked and that I was in real danger. I sat quietly waiting for cold steel at the back of my neck (or something else equally unpleasant). Silence. But the voice was so real that I knew something was going on. With a white-knuckle grip on the steering wheel I began to pray, Lord, please protect me in this situation.

A few seconds later I heard it again. I was given instructions to talk to three people about my relationship with the Lord. I was to encourage my mother to read her Bible. I was to encourage my younger brother to seek a relationship with Jesus; and I was to give my testimony to the guy I was dating at the time. Then there was no more voice.

I continued driving down the straight dark road towards Grand Forks. Obviously I was a bit distracted with my thoughts. But I wasn't worried because it was so late that the road was empty. Then I became physically distracted by flickering lights on the extreme right of my field of vision. The North Dakota horizon is very flat and the lights were very uncommon so I turned my head almost 90 degrees to my right to study the lights and try to figure out what they were all about. At the time this took place I was driving on the inside lane of a four-lane highway. Suddenly, to my complete surprise, the steering wheel jerked to the right and I was immediately in the outside lane of the highway. Before I had time to gather my wits and try to figure out what happened, headlights that I had not seen ahead of time whizzed by the driver's side of my car at a tremendous rate of speed. If my car had not changed lanes when it did I would have been involved in a head on collision. But, I didn't change lanes. In fact, I never saw the danger until it was passed.

At the edge of town, I pulled into the truck weigh station to report the car driving down the wrong side of the road. The station officer said he had just received a call about it from the police. They were pursuing a drunk driver who was driving on the wrong side of the road. They estimated his speed to have been about 70 mph.

I got back into my car to go home; but before I started the engine I prayed another short prayer . . . "Lord, I know you have spared my life for a reason. Please help me to understand what you ask of me." The next morning I questioned my memory of the night before. Did that incident really happen or was it only a vivid dream? The bruise on my thumb from where the steering wheel had been jerked out of my hand assured me it was no dream; and immediately I knew what I had to do. I picked up the phone and dialed . . . "Mom, we have to talk about this voice I heard last night . . .."

Review of this lesson

How do the angels interact with God? They reside in Heaven at the throne of God. They worship God, and do His bidding.

Do they serve Christ? Yes. They prophesied Christ's coming, serve Him, strengthened Him, worship Him, protect Him, and herald Him.

Are angels indwelled with the Holy Spirit? Probably not (No scriptures).

Do angels come in wrath? Yes.

Preview of the next five lessons

Lesson 8 – Who is Satan?

Lesson 9 – What about Satan's fall?

Lesson 10 – How does Satan interact with mankind?

Lesson 11 – Who are the fallen angels?

Lesson 12 – What are the activities of demons?

Preview of the next lesson

Who is Satan and how is he referred to in the Bible?

Lesson 8 - WHO IS SATAN?

Satan was the most beautiful of all the angels. This picture from Bible Readings for the Home, published by Pacific Press (Some images © 2003-2004 www.clipart.com, #84628) portrays Satan in all his splendor before his fall.

Review of the last lesson

Angels interact with God perpetually in Heaven at the throne of God, worshipping God, and doing His bidding.

They serve Christ throughout eternity. They prophesied Christ's coming, serve Him, strengthened Him, worship Him, protect Him, and herald Him.

Nothing is written in the Bible about angels being indwelled with the Holy Spirit? They are probably not since they are already confirmed in their holiness.

Angels have come and will come in wrath.

Review of the previous seven lessons

Lesson 1 - Introduction

We should remember to always seek Jesus, not angels.
Holy angels are real.

Lesson 2 – Who Are Holy Angels?

Lesson 3 – What are the traits of holy angels?

Lesson 4 – How do holy angels interact with humans?

Lesson 5 – Functions of holy angels with humans?

Lesson 6 – Organization of holy angels?

Lesson 7 – Functions of holy angels with God?

Preview of the next five lessons

The study of Satan and demons is important because we should know our enemy in order to fight him better. And this study will give us a greater appreciation of God's protective love for us.

Lesson 8 – Who is Satan?

Lesson 9 – What about Satan's fall?

Lesson 10 – How does Satan interact with mankind?

Lesson 11 – Who are the fallen angels?

Lesson 12 – What are the activities of demons?

Preview of this lesson

What are Satan's names?

What was Satan's nature in heaven?

What is his position among demons?

Is Satan powerful?

Does Satan have character attributes such as personality, or intellect?

Emotion? Will?

How is Satan referred to in the Bible?

Scriptures

Gen 3:1-2, 4, 13, 14 - Serpent (II Cor 11:3; Rev 12:9, 15, 20:2)

Isaiah 14:12-14 – O' morning star, son of the dawn! [day-star; son of the morning, Lucifer(KJV)] . . . King of Babylon

Ezek 28:11-14 - King of Tyre . . . anointed as a guardian cherub

Zech 3:1 - Satan (36 times)

Matt 4:3 - tempter (I Thes 3:5)

Matt 6:13 - evil one (Jn 17:15; II Thes 3:3; I Jn 5:18-19)

Matt 10:25 - *Baalzebub* (Matt 12:24, 27; Mark 3:; Lk 11:15, 18, 19

Matt 12:24 - prince of demons (Lk 11:15)

Jn 12:31 - prince of this world (Jn 14:30, 16:11)

II Cor 4:4 - god of this age

II Cor 6:15 - *Beliel*

II Cor 11:14 - angel of light

Eph 2:1-2 - ruler of the kingdom of the air, the spirit who is now at work in those who are disobedient

I Pet 5:8 - roaring lion

Rev 9:11 - angel of the Abyss . . . in Hebrew *Abbadon* and in Greek, *Appollyon*

Rev 12:9 - devil or Satan . . . leads the whole world astray (35 times)

Rev 12:3 - enormous red dragon

Rev 12:10: - accuser of the brethren

(FRUCHTENBAUM)[122]

Commentary

The Bible clearly teaches that Satan exists. This can be seen in three ways.

First of all Satan is mentioned in 7 of the 39 books of the Old Testament . . ..

Secondly, of the 27 books of the New Testament, Satan is mentioned in 19 of them . . ..

Thirdly, and very importantly, is that the existence of Satan was taught by Christ Himself. In the four gospels Satan is mentioned a total of 29 times. Of these 29, he is mentioned by Christ in 25. (FRUCHTENBAUM)[123]

Names . . .

Satan . . . is used 19 times in the Hebrew Old Testament . . . The Greek form of the name is *Satanas* . . . used 36 times in the Greek New Testament . . . means "adversary," or "resistor." This name emphasizes Satan as the leader of the rival kingdom to the Kingdom of God.

Devil . . . The Greek word is *diabolos* . . . used 35 times in the Greek New Testament . . . means "accuser," 'slanderer," or "one who trips up." This name pictures Satan as one who defames both God and the believer.

Beliel . . . means "worthlessness" and gives God's view of him now . . . .

Baalzebub . . . originates from the Hebrew *Baal Zvuv*, which literally means "the Lord of the Flies". He was the god of Ekron, a god of the Philistines, according to II Kings 1:2,3,6,16 . . . .. The Greek form is *Beelzebul* . . . means "the Lord of the Royal Palace" . . . the rabbis . . . changed his name to *Baalzebub* to poke fun at him.

Titles . . .

Day-star, son of the morning . . . .. It is extremely unfortunate that the King James Version translated it to the name "Lucifer." That name is not a translation of the Hebrew but a translation of a Latin term. "Lucifer" is the Latin translation of the Hebrew word which means day-star. But the correct reading in English should not be Lucifer, for that is never a biblical name for Satan or a biblical title . . . emphasizes him as being the shining one . . . how he was in his original state . . . .. He can still appear as an angel of light.

Destroyer . . . The Hebrew form is *Abbadon*, and the Greek form is *Appollyon* . . . .. He is the destroyer of both physical and spiritual life. There is a possibility that Revelation 9:11 is speaking of a chief demon rather than Satan.

Prince of this world . . . pictures Satan as carrying out his fifth I will to be like God.

Prince of the powers of the air . . . emphasizes Satan in his third and present abode—the atmospheric heavens. Secondly, it emphasizes him as being in authority over the other angels that fell with him.

God of this age . . . emphasizes the system of philosophy, which is contrary to God . . . the Satanic philosophy in the outworking of his control of the cosmos.

Evil one . . . his corrupted nature . . . the one who is the source of evil elsewhere.

Anointed cherub that covereth . . . First, it reveals of which order of celestial beings he belongs: he is a cherub. Secondly, it emphasizes his unique position—he was the anointed cherub that covereth. Other cherubs are holding the Throne of God . . . .. He was the one that served as the canopy over the Throne of God.

Prince of demons . . . emphasizes his authority over the one-third of the angels that fell with him.

King Tyre . . . he is in control over the earthly kingdoms of this world. King of Babylon . . . also emphasizes his control over nations.

Descriptions . . .

Accuser of the brethren . . . Whenever a believer falls into a state of unconfessed sin, sooner or later Satan will appear before the Throne of God, accusing that believer of that particular sin. This is why believers still need the ministry of Jesus as an advocate . . .. Satan not only accuses individual saints, but he is also the accuser of Israel as a nation before God.

Angel of light . . . emphasizes his deceptive character. It, too, is the outworking of the fifth I will: I will make myself like the Most High . . . appears as a counterfeit angel of light.

Tempter . . . one who entices to evil and as one who tries men in moral combat. He tempts people to commit acts of sin, in particular the sin of immorality.

Deceiver . . . he is continually going around deceiving . . . carrying out his fifth I will: I will make myself like the Most High.

Spirit that now works in the sons of disobedience . . .. This particular description emphasizes two things: first, that Satan is spirit being; and,

Secondly, as a spirit being he works among the children of men . . . among disbelievers. At one time all were in that category, but now believers have been redeemed from the Kingdom of Darkness into the Kingdom of the Son of God. So he no longer works in us, but he works against us.

Representation . . .

Serpent . . . emphasizes his craftiness . . . the most crafty of all personalities in the sinful state.

Great red dragon . . . emphasizes Satan in his power and in his ferocity.

The roaring lion . . . emphasis here is on his destructiveness; he is out to destroy. (FRUCHTENBAUM)[124]

"Satan" is a Hebrew word meaning "adversary," as "one to lie in wait"; hence, "the snares of the devil." In the New Testament, Satan is referred to under the name "Devil" (Greek: *diabolos*), meaning, "accuser, slanderer." The word "Devil" is not used in the Old Testament. It is *Abaddon* in Hebrew, *Apollyon* in Greek, meaning "destroyer." "Satan" and "Devil" are the two principal names used in the Scriptures, but there are a great number of appellations familiar to all Bible readers, namely: "the accuser of our brethren," "the evil one," "deceiver," "murderer," "father of lies," "*Beelzebub*," "*Belial*," "tempter," "great dragon," "serpent," "prince of demons," etc.—at least forty such titles are attributed to the fallen Lucifer. (EADE)[125]

What was Satan's position in heaven?
Scriptures
1. Ezek 28:12-19 - . . . lament concerning the king of Tyre: This is what the Sovereign LORD says: model of perfection, full of wisdom and perfect in beauty . . . in Eden . . . every precious stone adorned you: ruby, topaz and emerald, chrysolite, onyx and jasper, sapphire, turquoise and beryl. Your settings and mountings were made of gold; on the day you were created they were prepared . . . anointed as a guardian cherub, for so I ordained you . . . were on the holy mount of God; you walked among the fiery stones . . . blameless in your ways from the day you were created till wickedness was found in you. (NIV)

2. Jude 9 – . . . even the archangel Michael, when he was disputing with the devil about the body of Moses, did not dare to bring a slanderous accusation against him, but said, The Lord rebuke you! (NIV)

Commentary
Just like Michael was the archangel, the one in authority over all the other angels, Satan was the arch cherub, the one in authority over all the other cherubs. The cherubs are the highest order, and Satan, being the arch cherub, made him a higher category than Michael. (FRUCHTENBAUM)[126]

The most exalted of the angels, by creation and appointment, occupies the place of prominence in the Scriptures, second only to the Godhead. By his sin, the first created being to cross the will, the word and the purpose of the Creator, he became a devil . . . .. (EADE)[127]

While Scripture designates only Michael as an archangel (Jude 9), we have biblical grounds for believing that before his fall Lucifer was also an archangel, equal or perhaps superior to Michael.
Thus, we pick up the story where it began. It all started mysteriously with Lucifer. He was the most brilliant and most beautiful of all created beings in heaven. He was probably the ruling prince of the universe under God, against whom he rebelled. (GRAHAM)[128]

Concerning the origin of Satan this passage [Ezek 28:12-14] points out four things.
First of all when Satan was created he sealed up the sum in the two areas of wisdom and beauty . . . That means that of all created beings, Satan is by far the wisest of them all and the most beautiful of them all.

The second thing . . . is that he is a created being . . . first, he had a covering of stones which made him the shining one; and, secondly, he was in charge of the tablets and pipes, things involved in worship. So Satan, when he was created, served as one who led in heavenly worship of God who sat upon the Throne, and he is pictured as being the priest in heaven leading the worship of God.

The third thing . . . he was created a cherub . . . the anointed cherub . . . with this anointing Satan became the arch cherub—the one in authority over other cherubs . . ..

Fourth . . . he was perfect at the time of his creation . . . without a single flaw. He was so perfect that he had a unique ability—an ability called the power of contrary choice—the ability to choose contrary to one's nature.

He is of the first rank and this can be seen in three ways.

First, he was not just a cherub, but he was the anointed cherub . . ..

Secondly, even Michael had to respect him . . .. Thirdly, Satan is the leader over all fallen angels. (FRUCHTENBAUM)129

Seven things concerning the nature of Satan . . . a creature.
. . . a cherub. . . . of the first rank . . . even Michael had to respect him [Jude 8,9] . . . a spirit being; he is of celestial form . . . a confirmed sinner . . . ability to perform miracles . . . even to the point of the creation of life . . . it is dangerous to underestimate his abilities.
. . . a limited being . . .. (FRUCHTENBAUM)[130]

What is Satan's position among demons?
Scriptures
3. Matt 12:24 – . . . prince of demons . . .. (NIV) Lk. 11: 15
4. Rev 12:7-9 – . . . the dragon and his angels fought back. . . .. (NIV)

Does Satan have great power?
Scriptures
5. Job 1:12 - The Lord said to Satan . . . everything he has is in your hands, but on the man himself do not lay a finger. (Job 2: 6) (NIV)
6. Dan 10:12-14 - prince of the Persian kingdom resisted me twenty-one days. Then Michael . . . came to help me. (NIV)
7. Matt 7:22-23 – "Lord, Lord, did we not prophesy in your name, and in your name drive out demons and perform many miracles?" (NIV)
8. Eph 6:10-12 – Put on the full armor of God so that you can take your stand against the devil's schemes. (NIV)

9. II Thes 2:9-12 – . . . the work of Satan displayed in all kinds of counterfeit miracles, signs and wonders, and in every sort of evil that deceives those who are perishing. (NIV)

10. James 4:7 – Resist the devil, and he will flee from you. (NIV)

11. I Peter 5:8-9 – Resist him, standing firm in the faith. (NIV)

12. Rev 13:11-15 – And he performed great and miraculous signs, even causing fire to come down from heaven to earth in full view of men . . . on behalf of the first beast, he deceived the inhabitants of the earth . . .. He was given power to give breath to the image of the first beast, so that it could speak and cause all who refused to worship the image to be killed. (NIV)

Commentary

Do you not know that the prince of this world has been judged? He is not lord, nor prince any more. You have a different, a stronger, Lord, Christ, who has overcome and bound him. Therefore let the prince and god of this world look sour, bare his teeth, make a great noise, threaten, and act in an unmannerly way; he can do no more than a bad dog on a chain . . .. But because it is tied and you avoid it, it cannot bite you . . .. Therefore everything depends on this that we do not feel secure but continue in the fear of God and in prayer; then the chained dog cannot harm us . . .. Vicious dogs, as one observes, lie in wait and do not let themselves be heard. The power of the devil is not as great as it seems to be; for if he had the power to rage as he pleases, you would not live for an hour. (LUTHER)[131]

We are allowed a little glimpse of Satan's power in the Second Heaven from the account that is recorded in Daniel, Chapter 10. This passage gives the account of what happened when God assigned an angel to travel from the Third Heaven to earth to bring a message to the prophet Daniel. Satan did not want the message to reach Daniel, so he dispatched one of his princes to stop the angel from getting through. The angel was unable to get through alone, so he called upon the archangel to help him. (PITTMAN)[132]

He has the ability to perform miracles (II Thessalonians 2:9, Revelation 13:11-15). He does have tremendous miraculous powers, even to the point of the creation of life. That is why one must be very careful not to be convinced of the truth of something simply because of the existence of outward manifestations. Satan can duplicate a great number of miracles, and some of the miracles he duplicates are found in Matthew 7:22-23. So he has great miraculous powers, and it is dangerous to underestimate his abilities. He is a limited being; he does have limitations for he is a created being. This can be seen three ways. First he does not have the omni attributes. He is not omniscient, omnipresent, nor omnipotent. He may appear to have these three attributes and the reason is that Satan has a widespread network of demons, which make him appear to be omnipresent; his long experience in observing human responses to every trick and stimulus in every generation makes him appear to be omniscient; and, his power of miracles makes him appear to be omnipotent. But he is not omniscient, omnipotent or omnipresent; he does not have these attributes.

Secondly, God places limitations on what he can do. The best illustration of this is in Job 1-2 where God set the bounds for Satan and told him how far he would go and no more.

Thirdly, Satan can be resisted (Ephesians 6:10-18, James 4:7, I Peter 5:8-9). The fact that believers can resist him shows that Satan is a limited being. (FRUCHTENBAUM)[133]

Satan's power is limited by God's permissive will. Since Satan was cursed and doomed by God in the Garden of Eden, God has allowed Satan to have power on planet Earth—but it definitely is limited power. As a being created by God, everything Satan does must be allowed by the sovereign God, the creator.

Satan is limited by the extent of power God chooses to let him use. Satan is not omnipotent—only God is.

Satan also is limited by human will. God made all humans free moral agents. We have the right to choose to be transferred out of Satan's kingdom by accepting Jesus as Savior. And once we belong to Jesus, Satan can only tempt us—not make us fall. Satan is limited by time. He knows his time is limited before he will be cast into hell. His demons too know their time to harass people on earth will come to an end. (CHRISTENSON)[134]

Does Satan have a personality?
Scriptures
Does he have Intellect?

13. Gen 3:1-5 – Now the serpent was more crafty than any of the wild animals the LORD God had made. He said to the woman, "Did God really say, `you must not eat from any tree in the garden?'" . . . You will not surely die," the serpent said to the woman. "For God knows that when you eat of it your eyes will be opened, and you will be like God, knowing good and evil." (NIV)

14. Job 1-2 – (debates with God)

15. Matt 4:1-7 – The tempter came to him and said, if you are the Son of God, tell these stones to become bread. (NIV)

16. II Cor 11:3-4 – . . . just as Eve was deceived by the serpent's cunning, your minds may somehow be led astray from your sincere and pure devotion to Christ. (NIV)

Does he have emotions?

17. I Tim 3:6 – He must not be a recent convert, or he may become conceited and fall under the same judgment as the devil.

18. Rev 12:16-17 – . . . the dragon was enraged at the woman and went off to make war against the rest of her offspring. (NIV)

Does he have his own will?

19. Isa 14:12-14 – . . . I will ascend to heaven; I will raise my throne above the stars of God; I will sit enthroned on the mount of assembly, on the utmost heights of the sacred mountain. I will ascend above the tops of the clouds; I will make myself like the Most High. (NIV)

20. Luke 4:6-7 – The devil led him up to a high place . . . . And he said to him, I will give you . . . .. (NIV)

21. II Tim 2:25-26 – . . . that they will come to their senses and escape from the trap of the devil, who has taken them captive to do his will. (NIV)

Commentary

The devil can quote Scripture and deceive men with it. But his use of Scripture is defective. He does not quote it completely but only so much of it as serves his purpose. (LUTHER)[135]

Satan has intellect. For example in Job 1 and 2 he debates with God over the righteousness of Job, and that shows intellect. In Matthew 4:6 he is able to quote Scripture. In Luke 4:1-12 he is able to carry on a conversation with Jesus. In II Corinthians 11:3 he is described as being crafty, a function of intellect. In Ephesians 6:11 Paul spoke about the wiles of the devil and that, too, is a function of the intellect. Satan has the capacity to be puffed up—that is, to be filled with pride, and that is an emotion. Furthermore, Revelation 12:12,17 speaks of the wrath of Satan, which is the emotion of anger.

Satan also has will. For example, in Isaiah 14:13-14, five different times Satan declared I will. Luke 4:6-7 states that he has the power to give the Kingdoms of the World to whomsoever he wills. II Timothy 2:26 speaks of people being captivated into Satan's will. In I Peter 5:8, Peter speaks of Satan as one who is seeking whom he may devour. He is going around looking and choosing his victims, and his choice is made on the basis of his will. (FRUCHTENBAUM)[136]

Personal account

This is an account of a deaconess of a large evangelical church who had been born into a pagan Eastern religion and thought she had accepted Jesus several years before—but was not rid of all the evil beings still occupying her body. It was after midnight in the big empty meeting hall of a California mountain retreat center. Most of the lights had been turned out as those being counseled had trickled back into their bunks. All except this lady who had struggled for hours so insidiously with the demons of all those years. Alone with her in her deep distress, and completely naive as to what was happening, I held her in my arms while she identified, confessed, and denounced sin after sin. But with each one she denounced, she wretched and expelled long strings of gross matter from her nose. When the gruesome experience was finished, she trembled and then smiled with relief—and the two of us left that eerie scene to make our way through the blackness of night to our beds. But the next morning, beaming radiantly, she thanked me profusely for her new life in Jesus! (CHRISTENSON)[137]

Review of this lesson

What are some names of Satan? Serpent; morning star, son of the dawn! [day-star; son of the morning, Lucifer (KJV)] . . . King of Babylon; King of Tyre . . . anointed as a guardian cherub; Zech. 3: 1 - Satan; tempter; evil one; *Baalzebub*; prince of demons; prince of this world; god of this age; *Beliel*; angel of light; ruler of the kingdom of the air, the spirit who is now at work in those who are disobedient; roaring lion; angel of the Abyss . . . in Hebrew *Abbadon* and in Greek, *Appollyon*; devil or Satan . . . leads the whole world astray; enormous red dragon; and accuser of the brethren.

What was his nature in heaven? He was the model of perfection.

What is his position among demons? He is prince of demons.

Is he powerful? Limited by God, duplicates miracles, signs, wonders, can be resisted.

Does Satan have a Personality? Yes. Intellect? Yes, he debates with God and Jesus. He is crafty. He can quote scripture. He has a will.

Does he have emotions? Yes, puffed up, wrath. Does Satan have a will? He seeks to devour.

Mark R. Erickson

Preview of the next lesson
The next lesson will discuss Satan's fall and the result of that fall.

Lesson 9 - WHAT ABOUT SATAN'S FALL?

But, Satan's beauty was also his undoing as pride took over and he desired to become God. Satan is cast out of heaven as is depicted in this picture in Bible Reading for the Home, published by Pacific Press (Some images © 2003-2004 www.clipart.com, #84338). (I placed this picture crooked on purpose.)

Review of the previous lesson

Some references of Satan are: Serpent; morning star, son of the dawn! [daystar; son of the morning, Lucifer (KJV)], King of Babylon; King of Tyre . . . anointed as a guardian cherub; Zech 3:1 - Satan; tempter; evil one; *Baalzebub*; prince of demons; prince of this world; god of this age; *Beliel*; angel of light; ruler of the kingdom of the air, the spirit who is now at work in those who are disobedient; roaring lion; angel of the Abyss (in Hebrew *Abbadon* and in Greek, *Appollyon);* devil or Satan (leads the whole world astray); enormous red dragon; and accuser of the brethren.

Satan's was the model of perfection.

Satan is the prince of all demons.

Satan has power to duplicate miracles, signs, wonders, can be resisted and is limited by God.

Satan has individual personality through demonstrated intellect, emotion and will.

Preview of this lesson

Describe the fall.

What caused the fall?

What is Satan's domain?

What is the result of the fall?

How do Scriptures describe the fall of Satan?

Scriptures

1. Gen 1:3-10 – . . . Let there be light, and there was light. God saw that the light was good, and he separated the light from the darkness. God called the light "day," and the darkness he called "night." And there was evening, and there was morning—the first day . . . . God called the expanse "sky." And there was evening, and there was morning—the second day . . . . And God saw that it was good. (NIV)

2. Isa 14:12 – . . . You have been cast down to the earth, you who once laid low the nations! (NIV)

3. Ezek 28:16 – . . . I drove you in disgrace from the mount of God, and I expelled you. . . . (NIV)

4. Lk 10:18 – He replied, I saw Satan fall like lightning from heaven.

5. Rev 12:9 - That great dragon was hurled down—that ancient serpent called the devil or Satan. (NIV)

Commentary

For, even an angel had to live according to God and not according to an angel if he were to remain steadfast in the truth, speaking the truth out of God's grace and not lying out of his own weakness. And, once an angel rejected this Light, he became impure. Thus all those who were called unclean spirits were no longer light in the Lord but darkness in themselves, ...

. . . once we understand the creation of the angels by the making of the first light, then we should take the distinction between the good and bad angels as the meaning of the words: "God separated the light from the darkness, calling the light Day and the darkness Night."

We should not fail to notice that, in the Scripture, it was immediately after recording God's words, "Let there be light," and "there was light" that we are told: "God saw that the light was good." This was not said after He separated light from darkness and called the light day and the darkness night, lest it might appear that God testified to as much satisfaction in the darkness as in the light. It is different in the case of the darkness which is not evil and which is separated by the luminaries of heaven from the light we see with the eyes. The approval, "God saw that it was good," is here inserted, not before, but after, the division: "God set them in the firmament of the heavens to shed light upon the earth, to rule the day and the night and to separate the light from the darkness . . .. Both this kind of light and this kind of darkness pleased Him because both are without sin. (AUGUSTINE)[138]

Upon losing his princely appointment, "the anointed cherub" became Satan the adversary. The grandeur of his high office overwhelmed him with pride . . .. (EADE)[139]

But the important question is not, "When were angels created?" but, "When did they fall?" It is difficult to suppose that their fall occurred before God placed Adam and Eve in the Garden. We know for a fact that God rested on the seventh day, or at the end of all creation, and pronounced everything to be good. By implication, up to this time even the angelic creation was good. We might then ask, "How long were Adam and Eve in the Garden before the angels fell and before Satan tempted the first man and woman?" This question must remain unanswered. All we can say positively is that Satan, who had fallen before he tempted Adam and Eve, was the agent and bears a greater guilt because there was no one to tempt him when he sinned; on the other hand Adam and Eve were faced with a tempter.

The result was insurrection and war in heaven! He began a war that has been raging in heaven from the moment he sinned and was brought to earth shortly after the dawn of human history. It sounds like a modern world crisis! GRAHAM)[140]

What caused the fall?

Scriptures

6. Isa 14:13-14 – You said in your heart, I will ascend to heaven; I will raise my throne above the stars of God; I will sit enthroned on the mount of assembly, on the utmost heights of the sacred mountain. I will ascend above the tops of the clouds; I will make myself like the Most High. (NIV)

7. Ezek 28:15-17 – Your heart became proud on account of your beauty, and you corrupted your wisdom because of your splendor. So I threw you to the earth; I made a spectacle of you before kings. (NIV)

8. Jn 8:44 – . . . He was a murderer from the beginning, not holding to the truth, for there is no truth in him. When he lies, he speaks his native language, for he is a liar and the father of lies. (NIV)

9. I Jn 3:8 – . . . the devil has been sinning from the beginning. . . . (NIV)

Commentary

However, the joy of Eden was short-lived because of the proud and, therefore, envious spirit who fell from the heavenly Paradise when his pride caused him to turn away from God to his own self and the pleasures and pomp of tyranny, preferring to rule over subjects than be subject himself.

He could never have been blessed together with the other holy angels, since, refusing to be subject to his Creator, he took an arrogant joy in his own private sovereignty, thereby becoming a most deceitful liar . . . . From the moment of his creation the Devil refused the grace, which only a will devoutly obedient to God can receive. (AUGUSTINE)[141]

The statement in [Ezekiel 28] verse 15 is the closest the Bible ever comes to spelling out the origin of sin: unrighteousness was found in Satan. Somehow a perfect and holy being was found with unrighteousness . . . . He went from angel to angel trying to secure their allegiance by slandering God. One third of the innumerable number of angels were convinced by Satan and joined him . . . . This act of sin originated from the sin of pride; then the sin of slandering God led to violence—he caused violence in heaven by leading a revolt.

[Isaiah 14] With the first I will he desired to usurp God's Throne and sit on it himself in place of Christ . . . . With this [second] I will he expressed his desire to become the sole authority over each individual angel . . . . With this [third] I will Satan expressed his desire to become the messianic ruler over Israel himself . . .. Fourthly . . . "cloud" is used symbolically . . . of Shechinah Glory . . .. A glory that belongs only to God, is something Satan now desired for himself . . . Fifthly . . . With this [fifth] I will Satan expressed his desire to become sole possessor of everything that God created . . . to be like God in authority and power and control. (FRUCHTENBAUM)[142]

Pride was the thing that caused Lucifer's downfall, as definitely confirmed in the New Testament warning to young Christians . . . (I Timothy 3:6). Although the nature of Lucifer's sin is clearly disclosed, the question arises: "How could the principle of evil find welcome in a perfect and uninfluenced spirit-being, endowed with the privilege and responsibility of self-determination—God's irrevocable gift of "Free Will." The truth is: the creature, whether angel or man, is created to be God-centered—to become self-centered is the contradiction of the very purpose of the creature's existence. The only way this mighty angel could sin (as the Divine indictment reveals) is by centering his wisdom and understanding upon himself. Although high and mighty, Lucifer was capable of wrong self-determination, which led to apostasy, judgment and perdition. (EADE)[143]

Lucifer, the son of the morning, was created, as were all angels, for the purpose of glorifying God. However, instead of serving God and praising Him forever, Satan desired to rule over heaven and creation in the place of God. He wanted supreme authority! Lucifer said (Isaiah 14), "I will ascend into heaven." "I will exalt my throne above the stars of God." "I will sit also upon the mount of the congregation." "I will ascend above the heights of the clouds." "I will be like the most high." I . . . I . . . I . . . I . . .. Satan's desire to replace God as ruler of the universe may have been rooted in a basic sin that leads to the sin of pride I have already mentioned. Underneath Satan's pride lurked the deadliest of all sins, the sin of covetousness.

Today as always in the past, virtually no one can sin alone. The influences of sin are contagious. The Bible speaks of "the dragon . . . and his angels" (Revelation 12: 7), indicating that along with Lucifer, myriads of angels also chose to deny the authority of God and subsequently lost their high position. They chose to participate in the "war program" of Lucifer. (GRAHAM)[144]

Where is his domain?
Scriptures
10. Lk 4:5-7 - The devil . . . said to him, I will give you all their authority and splendor, for it has been given to me, and I can give it to anyone I want to. So if you worship me, it will all be yours. (NIV)

11. Jn 12:31 - . . . the prince of this world . . .. (NIV) (Jn 14:30, Jn 16: 8-11)

12. Eph 2:1-2 - . . . you were dead in your transgressions and sins, in which you used to live when you followed the ways of this world and of the ruler of the kingdom of the air, the spirit who is now at work in those who are disobedient. (NIV)

13. Eph 6:12 - . . . our struggle is not against flesh and blood, but against the rulers, against the authorities, against the powers of this dark world and against the spiritual forces of evil in the heavenly realms. (NIV)

14. Rev 12:12 - . . . But woe to the earth and the sea, because the devil has gone down to you! He is filled with fury, because he knows that his time is short. (NIV)

15. Rev 20:1-3 - . . . Abyss . . . bound him for a thousand years . . . threw him into the Abyss, and locked and sealed it over him, to keep him from deceiving the nations anymore until the thousand years were ended. After that, he must be set free for a short time. (NIV)

16. Rev 20:7-10 - When the thousand years are over, Satan will be released from his prison . . .. And the devil, who deceived them, was thrown into the lake of burning sulfur, where the beast and the false prophet had been thrown. They will be tormented day and night forever and ever. (NIV)

Commentary

The six abodes or dwelling places of Satan are the best way to trace his biography or his career.

Throne of God [Ezek 28:14] . . . while other cherubs are underneath the Throne, holding the Throne and supporting it, Satan was covering the Throne because he was the anointed cherub . . . he was also the guardian of God's Throne, so that he was the one that controlled who among the other angelic beings would have access to God.

Mineral Garden of Eden [Ezek 28:13] . . . not to be confused with the Garden of Eden . . . what this planet first looked like when it was originally created . . . the fall of Satan occurred.

Atmospheric heaven [Eph 2:2, 6:12] . . . Satan's current abode . . . he does have access to two other localities . . . into heaven [Job 1-2] . . . to be an accuser [Zech 3:1; Rev 12:10] . . . to the earth [Jn 12:31; II Cor 4:4] . . . as a roaring lion for the purpose of destruction [1 Pet 5:8-9] . . . an angel of light for the purpose of deception [II Cor 11:1-13].

The last three abodes of Satan are all future. Satan's present abode . . . will continue until the middle of the Tribulation. Then Satan will move into his fourth abode . . . confinement to earth [Rev 12:7-17] . . . for the second half of the Tribulation . . . Satan's main activity is going to be to try to annihilate the people of Israel.

Abyss [Rev 20:1-3] . . . that section of Sheol or Hades which is a temporary place of confinement for fallen angels. Satan will be confined there . . . for one thousand years.

Lake of Fire [Rev 20:7-10] . . . At the end of the Kingdom, Satan will be released from the abyss . . . for one last revolt against God's authority . . . . God will destroy them by fire out of heaven. At this point Satan will enter his . . . eternal abode forever and ever. (FRUCHTENBAUM)[145]

The first area in which Satan works is the cosmos . . . *kosmos*, which means "the world system. It is used 187 times in the Greek New Testament. (FRUCHTENBAUM)[146]

. . . *Aion*, which is used a total of 41 times. It is usually translated as "world" but a more literal rendering is "age" . . . in the sense of period of time . . . *oikoumenei*, also translated "world". It is used 14 times in the Greek New Testament . . . means "the inhabited world" . . . only those parts of the world that are inhabited by humanity . . ..

The one that concerns the relationship to Satan is *kosmos*. *Kosmos* is the world system which is under Satanic control . . .. The order system that is headed up by Satan and leaves God out . . . is anti- God in character . . . .. A vast order or system that Satan has promoted, which conforms to his ideals, aims, and methods, and includes government, conflict, armaments, jealousies, education, culture, religions of morality, and pride. This is the world that now exists (II Peter 3:5-7) It is what Satan employs, and this is a major area where Satan works. (FRUCHTENBAUM)[147]

Christ says that the devil is the prince of this world . . .. If, then, we would and must live upon earth, we must realize that we are guests and lodge in an inn with a knave as host and with an inscription or a sign over the door which reads "The House of Murder or The House of Lies."

Do not think that the devil is in hell, or beyond Babylon, or only in Turkey or at Rome with the Pope and his cardinal and bishops . . .. But here, among us, he is struggling and striving to turn us out of the heaven in which we are through Christ. (LUTHER)[148]

Sin appeared in the perfect, holy environment of heaven when Lucifer became proud and wanted to become like the most high God—and be worshipped by all. But no sin can stay there, so God cast Satan out of heaven. But, amazingly, God threw him not into hell—which was prepared for him—but to earth.

But Satan does not operate nor rule from hell now. He will be punished there, but that is in the future. His place of operation according to Ephesians 6:12 is "in the heavenly places." This is the sphere around planet Earth where the spiritual battle is raging today.

The "heavenly places" is not "heaven." Heaven is the place of abode of the Father, the only true God. (CHRISTENSON)[149]

The result of his fall concerning mankind

Scriptures

17. Gen 3:6-7 - . . . the eyes of both of them were opened, and they realized they were naked; so they sewed fig leaves together and made coverings for themselves. (NIV)

18. Isaiah 13:11-22 - I will punish the world for its evil, the wicked for their sins. I will put an end to the arrogance of the haughty and will humble the pride of the ruthless. I will make man scarcer than pure gold, more rare than the gold of *Ophir* . . . each will return to his own people, each will flee to his native land. Whoever is captured will be thrust through; all who are caught will fall by the sword. Their infants will be dashed to pieces before their eyes; their houses will be looted and their wives ravished . . .. Babylon, the jewel of kingdoms, the glory of the Babylonians' pride, will be overthrown by God like Sodom and Gomorrah. She will never be inhabited or lived in through all generations; no Arab will pitch his tent there, no shepherd will rest his flocks there. But desert creatures will lie there, jackals will fill her houses; there the owls will dwell, and there the wild goats will leap about. Hyenas will howl in her strongholds, jackals in her luxurious palaces. Her time is at hand, and her days will not be prolonged. (NIV)

19. Rom 5:12-14 - Therefore, just as sin entered the world through one man, and death through sin, and in this way death came to all men, because all sinned . . . death reigned from the time of Adam to the time of Moses, even over those who did not sin by breaking a command, as did Adam. (NIV)

20. 2 Cor 11:3 - . . . as Eve was deceived by the serpent's cunning, your minds may somehow be led astray from your sincere and pure devotion to Christ. (NIV)

21. Rev 12:9 - . . . leads the whole world astray. (NIV)

Commentary

This Lucifer, striving to insinuate his sly seductions into the minds of man whose fidelity he envied, since he himself had fallen, chose for his spokesman a serpent in the terrestrial Paradise, where all the animals of earth were living in harmless subjection to Adam and Eve . . .. He, at first parlayed cunningly with the woman as with the weaker part of that human society, hoping gradually to gain the whole. He assumed that a man is less gullible and can be more easily tricked into following a bad example than into making a mistake himself.

Moreover, our first parents only fell openly into the sin of disobedience because, secretly, they had begun to be guilty. Actually, their bad deed could not have been done had not bad will preceded it; what is more, the root of their bad will was nothing else than pride.

The Devil would not have begun by an open and obvious sin to tempt man into doing something which God had forbidden, had not man already begun to seek satisfaction in himself and, consequently, to take pleasure in the words: "You shall be as Gods."

Thus, there is a wickedness by which a man who is self-satisfied as if he were the light turns himself away from that true Light which, had man loved it, would have made him a sharer in the light; it was this wickedness which secretly preceded and was the cause of the bad act which was committed openly. (AUGUSTINE)[150]

We must, as I constantly say, allow Scripture to retain the simple, plain meaning supplied by the words and must provide no comments . . . . We must not direct it but must allow ourselves to be directed by it and accord it the honor of being put down better than we could express it. We must, therefore, let it stand that what the woman saw with her eyes was a real, natural serpent. (LUTHER)[151]

It was Satan who originated sin and he was the first sinner, . . . it was Satan who caused the fall of man. (FRUCHTENBAUM)[152]

Satan, the fallen prince of heaven, has made his decision to battle against God to the death . . . .. In his warfare against God, Satan uses the human race, which God created and loved. So understand God's forces of good and Satan's forces of evil have been engaged in a deadly conflict from the dawn of our history. Unless world leaders and statesmen understand the true nature of this warfare, they will continue to be blind leaders of the blind.

Lucifer became Satan, the devil, the author of sin; and it is sin that has always deceived, disturbed, betrayed, depraved and destroyed all that it had touched.

Satan and his demons are known by the discord they promote, the wars they start, the hatred they engender, the murders they initiate, the opposition to God and His commandments. They are dedicated to the spirit of destruction.

We live in a perpetual battlefield—the Great War of the Ages continues to rage. The lines of battle press in ever more tightly about God's own people. The wars among nations on earth are merely popgun affairs compared to the fierceness of battle in the spiritual, unseen world. This invisible spiritual conflict is waged around us incessantly and unremittingly.

Isaiah 13:12-14 clearly points up Satan's objectives: he works to bring about the downfall of nations, to corrupt moral standards and to waste human resources. Corrupting society's order, he wants to prevent the attainment of order, and to shake the kingdoms of our God. He uses his destructive power to create havoc, fire, flood, earthquake, storm, pestilence, disease and the devastation of peoples and nations.(GRAHAM)[153]

Personal account

My close friend Kathryn Grant also knows Satan is real. We were roommates as our group left the International Prayer Assembly in Seoul, Korea, to visit China in 1984. While many in our group had felt the evil that seemed to descend on us as we entered that country with its history of anti-God government, we were not prepared for the terror Kathryn experienced our first night there.

The day's events had set the stage, as she had been shocked at the reality of the filth and poverty of the communist's commune produced by a pagan regime. It brought back vivid memories of the first time she visited a pagan shrine as a new missionary in Japan and was overcome by the terrifying presence of evil she sensed . . .. Suddenly in the middle of the night Kathryn began to whisper from her bed, "Evelyn, Satan is in the room. Pray Evelyn, pray! Kathryn was not one given to dreams or hallucinations. After her missionary service, she had gone on to be a top executive in two large Christian organizations. That night in China, Satan really was there. Later, asking her to describe what Satan was like, she replied, "It was a black presence, like a tall human but no facial features. Definitely occupying space—the space on the right side of my bed, toward my feet. All around my bed was a black mist like a rectangular wall with clean-cut edges. But in my bed there was light. Satan was standing in the black mist. (CHRISTENSEN)[154]

Review of this lesson

Describe the fall of Satan. Separated, fallen, driven out, like lightening, hurled.

What caused the fall? Pride, 5 I wills.

What is Satan's domain? World, air, Abyss, Lake of Fire.

What is the result of the fall? Sin entered the world, war, and pestilence.

Preview of the next lesson

The next lesson will deal with how Satan interacts with mankind.

Lesson 10 - HOW DOES SATAN INTERACT WITH MANKIND?

Satan prowls the earth looking for a willing ear as is depicted in this picture from Pilgrim's Progress, published by Anson D. F. Randolph & Company (Some images © 2003-2004 www.clipart.com, #195990).

Review of the previous lesson

Satan and his angels were separated, fallen, driven out, like lightening, hurled down.

Pride (five I wills) caused the fall.

Satan exists in the world, air, Abyss, Lake of Fire.

Because of the fall sin entered the world, war, pestilence.

Satan's defeat was prophesied. He is already defeated by the cross.

Preview of this lesson

Does Satan have power over death?

What are some other activities of Satan among unbelievers?

How does Satan interact with believers?

Does Satan have power over death?

Scriptures

1. Heb 2:14-15 – . . . him who holds the power of death—that is, the devil . . .. (NIV)

2. I Jn 5:16-17 – . . . There is a sin that leads to death. (NIV)

Commentary

All sadness is of the devil, for he is the lord of death. At all hours the devil is seeking to kill us all. After you have been baptized he will not let you have any rest. If he could kill you in your mother's body, he would do it. He is not satisfied to let us have one kernel of grain on the field, one fish or piece of bread, or anything good. Far less does he spare us who are exposing his shame, who rebuke him to his face, and preach what we should—God's grace and the works of the devil. Satan knows that we must die. Nevertheless, he is so very furious against us that, so far as he is concerned, he would bring about our death any minute and would do so from the beginning of our life.

The devil reminds me of a bird catcher. Usually he slaughters all he catches. But if he has a bird that pleases him, he permits it to live that it may sing whatever its captor pleases.

Whatever therefore pertains to death is the handiwork of the devil; and, conversely whatever pertains to life is the blessed work of God. (LUTHER)[155]

He has power over death in relationship to unbelievers. Throughout the history of the Old Testament, Satan had the power of death both in relationship to believers and unbelievers. But when Jesus, died, He entered into the realm of death; He then passed through death and took away the keys of death from Satan insofar as believers are concerned. Satan no longer has authority over the death of believers, except in one case, which will be discussed later.

He applies physical death for a believer who has been excommunicated (I Corinthians 5:5). As mentioned earlier, as a result of the work of Christ— through His death and resurrection—Jesus took away the keys of death from Satan as far as believers are concerned . . .. The one exception is in the case of a believer who has undergone the four steps of church discipline mentioned in Matthew 18:15-20. The final step is excommunication, which means that he is put back into Satan's domain for the destruction of the flesh, and Satan then has the authority to put that excommunicated believer to death. The verse goes on to teach that this will not affect the believer's salvation. The believer will still be saved, but he will have an untimely death and will not fulfill the calling of God in his own life. This is also the sin unto death that John speaks of in I John 5:16. (FRUCHTENBAUM)[156]

Other activities of Satan among unbelievers
Scripture:

3. Matt 13:19 – When anyone hears the message about the kingdom and does not understand it, the evil one comes and snatches away what was sown in his heart. (NIV)

4. Mk 4:15 – Satan comes and takes away the word that was sown in them. (NIV)

5. Lk 8:11-12 – . . . the devil comes and takes away the word from their hearts, so that they may not believe and be saved. (NIV)

6. Lk 13:16 – . . . daughter of Abraham, whom Satan has kept bound for eighteen long years

7. Acts 10:38 – . . . healing all who were under the power of the devil. (NIV)

8. Acts 13:8-10 – . . . looked straight at Elymas and said, "You are a child of the devil and an enemy of everything that is right! You are full of all kinds of deceit and trickery. Will you never stop perverting the right ways of the Lord"? (NIV)

9. II Cor 4:3-4 – . . . our gospel is veiled, it is veiled to those who are perishing. The god of this age has blinded the minds of unbelievers, so that they cannot see the light of the gospel of the glory of Christ, who is the image of God. (NIV)

10. Eph 2:1-2 – . . . you were dead in your transgressions and sins, in which you used to live when you followed the ways of this world and of the

ruler of the kingdom of the air, the spirit who is now at work in those who are disobedient. (NIV)

11. I Jn 2:15-17 – Do not love the world or anything in the world. If anyone loves the world, the love of the Father is not in him. For everything in the world . . . comes not from the Father but from the world. (NIV)

12. I Tim 4:1-8 – . . . in later times some will abandon the faith and follow deceiving spirits and things taught by demons. Such teachings come through hypocritical liars, whose consciences have been seared as with a hot iron. (NIV)

13. I John 4:1-3 - . . . do not believe every spirit, but test the spirits to see whether they are from God, because many false prophets have gone out into the world . . . but every spirit that does not acknowledge Jesus is not from God. This is the spirit of the antichrist, which you have heard is coming . . . is already in the world. (NIV)

Commentary

Satan's ideology is based on the little word "if." Through all time he has sought to discredit God by making Him out a liar in the eyes of man. He never ceases trying to discredit the claims of the Word of God and to rob mankind of the strength and comfort of faith. The all-time tool of Lucifer is an "if," but God declares that there are no "ifs," "buts" or "ands" about His program for salvation. God's plan is unalterable; His antidote for the satanic "if" works and is unchangeable.

Listen to Satan's "ifs" of death being injected into the minds of people today: "if" you live a good life, "if" you do what is right, "if" you go to church, "if" you work for the benefit of others—if, if, if. But the Bible teaches that these "ifs" are not enough to meet God's requirements for salvation . . . .. Only when we turn to Christ in faith and trust, confessing our sins to Him and seeking His forgiveness, can we be assured of our salvation. Satan will do all in his power to make us trust ourselves instead of Christ. (GRAHAM)169

When God's holy Word arises, it is always its lot that Satan opposes it with all his might . . . .. What he is unable to crush by force he thus seeks to suppress by cunning and lies. (LUTHER)[157]

The Hebrews were brought into contact with the surrounding nations who paid homage to numerous deities. The root abomination of idolatry was Demonism Divination. The inordinate desire to penetrate the future and the unseen created one of the oldest arts in the realm of the occult.

A consulter with evil spirits. Divination has many and varied forms. A consulter with evil spirits denotes one possessed of a soothsaying demon, such as the girl at Philippi (Acts 16:16-18).

Necromancer—from *nekros*, a "dead body," and *manteia*, "divination." One who interrogates the dead. The Bible shows clearly that the dead do not return or reveal their secrets to men. Thus, it is evident that Satan and his angels (messengers), designated "demons," are the real operators in any attempted intercourse with the unseen world on behalf of the living (Isaiah 8: 19).

Witchcraft. The word "witch" denotes "a knowing one." The word translated "witchcraft" in the Authorized Version (Galations 5:20) is the Greek word for 'sorcery," *pharmakeia*, which is associated with the giving of magical potions.

Missionaries witnessing in lands where similar phenomena still exist testify that the power of demonism is overwhelming. (EADE)[158]

First, he tries to prevent unbelievers from accepting and believing the Gospel. Wherever the Gospel is proclaimed, Satan or his agents will be out there trying to keep people from believing it. He does this in two ways.

First, he tries to snatch the Gospel seed sown in the hearer (Matthew 13:19, Mark 4:15, Luke 8:13).

Secondly, Satan tries to prevent acceptance of the Gospel by blinding the mind of the unbeliever, so when the Gospel is presented the unbeliever does not comprehend exactly what the issuers are (II Corinthians 4:3-4).

He promotes attraction to falsehood. This he does in two ways.

First, he indoctrinates people into false religious systems. He teaches them false doctrines that they can be satisfied with (I Timothy 4:1-3, I John 4:1-4).

A second way he promotes attraction to falsehood is by teaching a false lifestyle as described in Ephesians 2: 1-3 and I John 2:15-17.

He causes suffering and oppression. Not all suffering and oppression is caused by Satan, but sometimes it is (Luke 13:16, Acts 10:38).

He uses unbelievers to pervert the Gospel (Acts 13:8-10).

He energizes his own ministers. He has his own ministers that he produces, fills and controls . . . .. These ministers of Satan fashion themselves to sound like and seem like real ministers of Christ in order to carry out his work of deception. According to II Corinthians 11:13-15, these ministers of Satan are not the obvious type, like those who head up the churches of Satan, but ministers that fashion themselves to appear as ministers of Christ.

He uses unbelievers to oppose the Gospel in various ways, active or passive (Revelation 2:9,13). (FRUCHTENBAUM)[159]

How does Satan interact with believers?

Tempts us:

Scriptures

14. Matt 4:1-10 - . . . Jesus was led by the Spirit into the desert to be tempted by the devil. (NIV)

15. Acts 5:3-4 – . . . Peter said, Ananias, how is it that Satan has so filled your heart that you have lied to the Holy Spirit and have kept for yourself some of the money you received for the land? (NIV)

16. I Cor 7:5 – . . . come together again so that Satan will not tempt you because of your lack of self-control. (NIV)

17. I Thes 3:5 – . . . I was afraid that in some way the tempter might have tempted you and our efforts might have been useless. (NIV)

Commentary

Sadness in our relation to God is most certainly the work of the devil. When, therefore he suggests an evil thought to you about God, as if God did not want to have mercy on you but wanted you to perish and die; or when he instills into you this notion: Right now you must die, then quickly conclude that it is diabolical, not a divine suggestion . . . . But Satan does not like to let such pious thoughts about God and Christ come to us during temptations. He obscures these thoughts and keeps them away. The human heart is then so obsessed with the Law, sin, and death that it does not admit the article of justification and faith . . . .

The devil takes no holiday; he never rests. If beaten, he rises again. If he cannot enter in front, he steals in at the rear. If he cannot enter in the rear, he breaks through the roof or enters by tunneling under the threshold. He labors until he is in. He uses great cunning and many a plan.

God sends no sickness into the world but through the devil. All sadness and sickness are of the devil, not of God. For God permits the devil to harm us because He receives little regard from us.

God allows pestilence, war, or some other plague to come, that we may humble ourselves before Him, fear Him, hold to Him, and call upon Him. When God has accomplished these purposes through the scourge, then the good angels come again to perform their office. (LUTHER)[160]

Satan tempts believers (I Thessalonians 3:5). This is a major work of Satan among believers, and he tempts them in at least six areas.

First, he tempts believers to lie (Acts 5:3).

Secondly, he tempts believers to commit sexual sins (I Corinthians 7:5) . . . .

Thirdly, Satan tempts believers to commit specific acts of sin (I Peter 5:8).

Fourthly he tempts believers to be preoccupied with the things of the world (I John 2:15-17, 5:19).

Fifthly, Satan tempts believers to develop pride in spiritual matters, and in that way the believer falls into the same sin that brought about the fall of Satan (I Timothy 3:6).

Sixthly, he tempts believers to rely on human wisdom and strength rather than on divine wisdom (I Chronicles 21:1-8). (FRUCHTENBAUM)[161]

Accuse us before God:
Scriptures
18. Rev 12:10 – . . . the accuser of our brothers, who accuses them before our God day and night, has been hurled down. (NIV)

Commentary
Devil is a Greek name meaning calumniator, a criminal, slanderer, and reviler. That is the devil's office according to scripture; he is one who speaks the worst of you and me . . .. Nor, is the devil satisfied with slander, but he also defiles what is good and even turns it into evil.

Is it not a plague that wretch, the devil, wants to accuse and judge us and is himself worse than all human beings?

The wickedness of the devil is so great that no man can grasp it, nor is it possible for any human being to be so wicked in his own nature.

When the devil attacks a man, he makes heaven and earth too narrow for him. At times he plagues me, too, to such a degree that he converts a pardonable sin into an ocean and a fire so vast that I do not know which way to turn. (LUTHER)[162]

He [Michael] said, "In case you are not aware of it, twenty-four hours a day there is some type of evil force accusing God's people of things he has already forgiven." Satan does not see things the way God sees them. He knows they are forgiven, but he keeps on accusing them anyway. (BUCK)[163]

Appears righteous:
Scriptures
19. Mat 24:4-5 – For many will come in my name, claiming, `I am the Christ," and will deceive many. (NIV)

20. 2 Cor 11:12-15 – . . . Satan himself masquerades as an angel of light. It is not surprising, then, if his servants masquerade as servants of righteousness. (NIV)

Commentary

Satan came to me and told me he was God. He attempted to persuade me to surrender my will to live. In deception, he tried to kill my physical body through my own sovereign will.

I heard the most beautiful voice. There were no words in earthly vocabulary that could remotely describe the sound I heard. It was the most beautiful thing I had ever experienced in this world and just by the tone of the voice, the speaker implied he was God. (PITTMAN)[164]

Satan sometimes "transforms himself into an angel of light," in order to test those who need testing or to deceive those deserving deception, nothing but the great mercy of God can save a man from mistaking bad demons for good angels, and false friends for true ones, and from suffering the full damages of this diabolical deception, all the more deadly in that it is wily beyond words. (AUGUSTINE)[165]

Where the names of God and of Christ are used, everybody follows, imagines that the cause is altogether divine, and goes to the devil with it. For it must be that the world is deceived and misled by the use of God's name . . .. For the devil cannot sell his lies but under this beloved name; therefore he must embellish them with a fine appearance and gloss them over with these holy names: God's Word, the worship of God, a divine life, etc. . . .. Therefore, we must be warned to be on our guard and not to be deceived, but to hear His Word, spoken here and at other times, and judge and decide in accordance with it alone.

Let us learn clearly to recognize the tricks and subtleties of the devil. No heretic comes in the name of error or Satan, or does the devil himself come as devil, especially not the white one. Nay, even the black devil, when he impels a man to commit obviously shameful sins, provides him with a covering, enabling him to belittle the sin he is about to commit or is committing . . .. But in spiritual matter not the black but the white devil operates and presents himself in angelic and divine guise.

The white, good-looking devil is the one who does the most harm, the devil who eggs people on to commit spiritual sins, which are not regarded as sins at all but as pure righteousness and are defended as such. A popular proverb has it: Where God builds a church, the devil builds a tavern next door.

The devil forever desires to imitate God . . .. He cannot bear to see God speaking. If he cannot prevent it nor hinder God's Word by force, he opposes it with a semblance of piety, takes the very words, which God has spoken, and so twists them as to peddle his lies and poison under their name. This strategy becomes an occasion for stumbling to many people and at times misleads even those who have and know God's Word. (LUTHER)[166]

It is the same Satan who, disguising himself as an angel of light (2 Corinthians 11:14), fools us into believing that "it can't be sin if it fulfills our needs," who fools our children into believing the Satanic rock and roll is just "modern music," who deceives our teens into believing "suicide is a good and honorable way out of problems." (CHRISTENSON)[167]

Other activities in relation to believers:
Scriptures

21. Job 1:6-12, 2:1-6 – One day the angels came to present themselves before the LORD, and Satan also came with them. The LORD said to Satan, "Where have you come from"? Satan answered the LORD, "from roaming through the earth and going back and forth in it." Then the LORD said to Satan, "Have you considered my servant Job? There is no one on earth like him; he is blameless and upright, a man who fears God and shuns evil. Does Job fear God for nothing"? Satan replied. "Have you not put a hedge around him and his household and everything he has? You have blessed the work of his hands, so that his flocks and herds are spread throughout the land. But stretch out your hand and strike everything he has, and he will surely curse you to your face." The LORD said to Satan, "Very well, then, everything he has is in your hands, but on the man himself do not lay a finger." (NIV)

22. Lk 22:31-34 – "Simon, Simon, Satan has asked to sift you as wheat. (NIV)

23. 1 Cor 5:1-5 – . . . reported that there is sexual immorality among you, and of a kind that does not occur even among pagans: A man has his father's wife. And you are proud! Shouldn't you rather have been filled with grief and have put out of your fellowship the man who did this? Even though I am not physically present, I am with you in spirit. And I have already passed judgment on the one who did this, just as if I were present. . . . hand this man over to Satan, so that the sinful nature may be destroyed and his spirit saved on the day of the Lord. (NIV)

24. II Cor 2:5-11 – . . . I have forgiven in the sight of Christ for your sake, in order that Satan might not outwit us. For we are not unaware of his schemes. (NIV)

25. II Cor 11:1-14 – . . . Satan himself masquerades as an angel of light. It is not surprising, then, if his servants masquerade as servants of righteousness. Their end will be what their actions deserve. (NIV)

26. II Pet 2:1-9 – . . . there were also false prophets among the people, just as there will be false teachers among you. They will secretly introduce destructive heresies, even denying the sovereign Lord who bought them—bringing swift destruction on themselves. Many will follow their shameful ways and will bring the way of truth into disrepute. In their greed these teachers will exploit you with stories they have made up. Their

condemnation has long been hanging over them, and their destruction has not been sleeping. (NIV)

27. II Cor 12:7 – . . . there was given me a thorn in my flesh, a messenger of Satan, to torment me. (NIV)

28. I Thes 2:18 – . . . we wanted to come to you . . . but Satan stopped us. (NIV)

29. II Thes 2:9 – The coming of the lawless one will be in accordance with the work of Satan displayed in all kinds of counterfeit miracles, signs and wonders, and in every sort of evil that deceives those who are perishing. . . . they refused to love the truth and so be saved. For this reason God sends them a powerful delusion so that they will believe the lie and so that all will be condemned who have not believed the truth but have delighted in wickedness. (NIV)

30. I Tim 1:19-20 – . . . Some have rejected these and so have shipwrecked their faith. (NIV)

31. I Tim 3:7 – He must also have a good reputation with outsiders, so that he will not fall . . . the devil's trap. (NIV)

32. II Tim 2:24-26 – And the Lord's servant must not quarrel; instead, he must be kind to everyone, able to teach, not resentful. Those who oppose him he must gently instruct, in the hope that God will grant them repentance leading them to a knowledge of the truth, and that they will come to their senses and escape from the trap of the devil, who has taken them captive to do his will. (NIV)

33. I Pet 5:8-9 – Be self-controlled and alert. Your enemy the devil prowls around like a roaring lion looking for someone to devour. (NIV)

34. Rev 2:10 – I tell you, the devil will put some of you in prison to test you, and you will suffer persecution for ten days. Be faithful, even to the point of death, and I will give you the crown of life. (NIV)

Commentary

Satan controls some believers from within. The worst term ever used in trying to describe this control is "possession", because the Greek word for possession is never actually used. The Greek word is always a word that means "to be controlled from within; or "demonized". Yes, believers can be controlled from within. For example, in Acts 5:3 Satan filled Ananias and Sapphira, and Peter used the very same words there that Paul used in Ephesians 5:18 where he said: . . . be filled with the Spirit. To be filled is to be controlled from within, and Satan was controlling them from within. Paul, in Ephesians 4:27, admonishes not to give a place to the devil. Greek word for "place" is a military term that means a "beachhead". Do not give a beachhead to the devil.

First, he sifts believers the way he sifted Peter. The result of the sifting of Peter by Satan was Peter's denial of Jesus (Luke 22:31)

He hinders believers from accomplishing their calling (I Thessalonians 2:18).

He gains advantage over some believers who allow themselves to be deceived (II Corinthians 2:11).

He beguiles some believers, as he did Eve (II Corinthians 11:3).

He buffets believers, as he did in the case of Paul (II Corinthians 12:7).

Satan wars against the saints (Ephesians 6:10-18), which is why believers need to wear the armor of God.

He accuses and slanders believers before the Throne of God (Revelation 12:10).

He plants doubts in believers' minds about the truth of God and the veracity of God, as he did to Eve (Genesis 3:1-5).

Satan incites persecution against believers (Revelation 2:10).

Satan infiltrates the church in two ways. One way is with false disciples (the tares of Matthew 13:38-39). Secondly, he infiltrates the church with false teachers who preach another Jesus of the same kind (II Corinthians 11:13-15, II Peter 22:1-19).

Satan promotes division in the church and many churches are split because of satanic influence (II Corinthians 2:1-11).

He devours believers and that means he gets believers so deeply into sin that they sometimes never get out (I Peter 5:8).

Satan is responsible for shipwrecking the faith of some believers, where they totally lose their faith (I Timothy 1:19-20). Fortunately, even then they don't lose their salvation.

Satan employs his demons to try to defeat the saints (Ephesians 6:10-12).

Satan even misuses Scripture. He can and does quote Scripture correctly, but he misuses it in that he either quotes it out of context or he gives a misapplication as he tried to do with Jesus (Matthew 4:5-6, Luke 4:9-11).

Satan uses four specific procedures against believers. First, he uses devices and special designs to entrap the believer (II Corinthians 2:11).

Secondly, he uses wiles (Ephesians 6:11). Thirdly, he puts out snares (I Timothy 3:7, II Timothy 2:26). Fourthly, he uses miracles as lying wonders. He does have the power of miracles and he does use this for the purpose of working against the saints (II Thessalonians 2: 9). (FRUCHTENBAUM)[168]

There are Christians who feel the Bible's 1 John 4:4 promise . . . is their automatic insulation against any victories of the devil without their doing anything. And many believe when Jesus came to live in them at salvation, which He did, their battle with Satan ceased. But just the opposite is true.

In fact, the battle with Satan only starts when we become Christians. Before that, we are members of Satan's domain darkness—and certainly are not at war with him. The call to put on armor is the Christians' summons to prepare for conflict—a war that has been raging since the Garden of Eden.

When we Christians enter the battle to rescue souls, we automatically escalate Satan's attacks on us. As long as we don't threaten his kingdom, he doesn't worry too much about us. But when we obey Jesus and get into the battle for souls, we must strengthen our defensive stance against Satan and be strong in the Lord. This is why God provided armor for us. (CHRISTENSON)[169]

Personal Account

I learned quite by accident in the early '70s, how to fight *offensively* with Satan for souls. I was doing a Bible study series in the Minnetonka Baptist Church and had asked if anyone wanted to accept Jesus. Several prayed with the usual joy of becoming a new creation in Jesus. All except one. Hilarie (named changed) tried to pray, but couldn't. So I invited her to stay with me after the others had left. Alone in a little room we knelt to pray. I expected the same response as usual; but, to my amazement, she absolutely could not pray asking Jesus into her heart. She tried and tried, but would look at me with anguish in her eyes and cry, "I can't!" Then she would try again. And I would pray. And she would pray. She went limp as she dropped her head on the chair where she was kneeling. She could not accept Jesus.

Suddenly a light dawned. I felt an unbelievable anger toward Satan surge over me. How did he have the audacity to keep my class member out of Jesus' kingdom? I spewed out my condemnation of him—directly to him. (It was not prayer. I do not pray to Satan. I was just telling him off in no uncertain terms.) "Satan," I snapped, "you have no right to do this to Hilarie. I claim the *blood* and the *name of Jesus of Nazareth* against you. You *must* leave. You have absolutely no right to hinder her any longer. Jesus died and shed His blood for her. He already has bought her back from you. You *must* leave. Immediately something seemed to pop. The bondage was gone. She was free. With ease she prayed asking Jesus to be her Lord and Savior. She was radiant as she lifted her tear-stained face to mine, beaming a great big smile. Free in Jesus! (CHRISTENSON)[170]

Review of this lesson

Does Satan have power over death? Possibly only in unbelievers.

How does Satan interact with unbelievers? Blocking acceptance/believing, falsehoods, suffering/oppression, sow unbelievers among believers, pervert Gospel, own Christ-like ministers, oppose Gospel, death.

How does Satan interaction with believers? Temptation, accusation, appears righteous, sift, hinder calling, strife, dissension, deception, test, confuse.

Preview of the next lesson

The next lesson will discuss fallen angels.

Lesson 11 - WHO ARE THE FALLEN ANGELS (DEMONS)?

What do demons look like? Who knows. These are examples of one person's idea, Pieter Huys, in the Treasury of Fantastic & Mythological Creatures, published by Dover Publications (Some images © 2003-2004 www.clipart.com, #956379, #956383, #956399, and #956409).

Note:
Much of the study of fallen angels is repetitive of their chief, Satan, since they do his bidding. Although, I have tried to avoid repetition, out of necessity, some areas of study will overlap.

Review of the previous lesson

Satan has power over death, possibly only in unbelievers.

Satan Interacts with unbelievers by: blocking acceptance/ believing, falsehoods, suffering/oppression, sow unbelievers among believers, pervert Gospel, own Christ-like ministers, oppose Gospel, death

Satan Interacts with believers using: Temptation, accusation, appearing righteous, sifting, hinder calling, strife, dissension, deception, testing, confusing.

Preview of this lesson

Names of demons
When did they fall? How many? Are they organized?
In hell?

How are demons referred to in the Bible?

Scriptures

Gen 6:1-4 - sons of God (1 time)
Deut 18:10-11 - *familiar spirit, medium or spiritualist (3 times)
Deut 32:17 - *shedim, to rule or to be lord (2 times)
Lev 17:7 - *seirim, goat idols (4 times)
I Sam 16:14-16 - *evil spirit (4 times)
I Kgs 22:21-22 - *lying spirit (1 time)
Ps 78:49 - *angels of evil (1 time)
Ps 91:6 - *ketev, destroys (1 time)
Ps 96:5 - *elilim, idols(1 time)
Isa 34:14 - *lilit, night creatures, night demons (1 time)
Isa 65:11 - *gad, Fortune, *meni*, Destiny (Fate) (1 time)
Matt 4:24 - *daimonizomai, to be controlled by a demon from within (13 times)
Matt 8:28-31 - *daimon, evil power (1 time)
Matt 10:1 - *Unclean spirit (8 times)
Matt 25:41 - *angels (2 times)
Lk 4:33 - *daimonion, demon (63 times)

Lk 7:21 - *evil spirit (2 times)
Lk 11:26 - *wicked spirit (1 time)
Acts 17:22 - *deisidaimones-teros, to be very reverent to Demons (1 time)
Acts 25:19 - *deisdamonis, demon worship (1 time)
I Tim 4:1 - *seducing spirit (1 time)
James 3:15 - *daimoniodes, demonical (1 time)
Rev 9:11 - Heb. = Abaddon, Gk. = Apollyon, destruction (1 time)
Rev 16:13 - *spirit of demons (1 time)
*(FRUCHTENBAUM)[171]

Commentary

The English word "demon" comes from the Greek word *daimonia* . . . is used sixty times in the New Testament. The existence of demons is mentioned by every New Testament writer except by the author of Hebrews who did mention Satan.

Jesus positively taught that demons do exist . . . cast out demons the disciples recognized the existence of demons

    . . . twelve Old Testament names . . ..
    . . . angels of evil . . . messengers of Satan who is called the Evil One.
    . . . sons of God . . . good angels, but it can also refer to evil angels.
    . . . *seirim*, which refers to demons that have the form of a goat . . .
    . . . *lilit* . . . demons of the night.
    . . . *shadim* . . . to rule or to be lord.
    . . . evil spirit . . ..
    . . . lying spirit . . ..
    . . . familiar spirit . . . witches, spiritualists . . ..
    . . . *gad* which means fortune.
    . . . *meni* which means fate.
    . . . *elilim* . . . demons of idolatry.
    . . . *ketev* . . . involved in the work of destruction.
    . . . four categories of names found in the New Testament.
    . . . demon is "intelligence" . . . daimon which means "evil power" . . *daimonion* . . . most basic word for demon and is used 63 times . . . *daimoniodes* which means "demonical," . . . *daimonizomai* which means "to be controlled by a demon from within.;" It is used a total of 13 times . . . *deisidaimones-teros*, which means "to be very reverent to demons." It emphasizes the occult world. . . . *deisdamonis*, which means "demon worship." It, too, is strongly connected with the occult world.

    spirit . . . is used a total of 46 times in conjunction with demons . . . evil spirit . . . unclean spirit . . . wicked spirit . . . seducing spirits . . . spirits of demons.

    angels . . . Satan's angels.
    destruction . . . the demon of the Abyss. (FRUCHTENBAUM)[172]

When did the demons fall? How many? Organized?

Scriptures

1. Mk 5:9 - My name is Legion, for we are many. (NIV)
2. Rev 12:3-4a - . . . swept a third of the stars out of the sky and flung them to the earth. (NIV)
3. Rev 12:9 - The great dragon was hurled down . . .. He was hurled to the earth, and his angels with him. (NIV)

Commentary

Let it, then suffice for us to know that there are good and evil angels, but that God created them all equally good. Thence it follows of necessity that the evil angels fell and did not stand firm in the truth. But how this happened is not known. However, it is very probable that they fell by pride, because they despised the Word, or the Son of God, and wanted to exalt themselves above Him.

Differences exist among the good angels as well as among the devils . . . for this is the very reason why Christ says that they have a kingdom. (LUTHER)[173]

There are several indications that there are a great number of demons. What is obvious is that the organization of demons is an imitation of the organization of elect angels with similar ranks and orders. (FRUCHTENBAUM)[174]

The spirits called angels were never, in any sense, at any time, partakers of darkness, but, from the moment of their creation, they were made beings of light . . .. Some angels, however, turned away from this illumination and failed to attain this eminence of wisdom and blessedness which is unthinkable apart from the possession and assurance of everlastingness.

I know it may seem difficult to believe that, while the angels were so created that some were in ignorance concerning their perseverance or defection and others were infallibly assured of the eternity of their bliss, yet all were created from the beginning equally blessed and remained so until the angels who are now evil fell voluntarily from their light and love.

What "makes" the will evil is, in reality an "unmaking," a desertion from God . . .. Thus, the reason why the bad were separated from the society of good angels was that the good persevered in the same good will, whereas the others changed themselves into bad angels by defection from good will. The only thing that "made" their will bad was that they fell away from a will, which was good. Nor would they have fallen away, had they not chosen to fall away.

The contrary dispositions which have developed among these good and bad angels are due, not to different natures and origins, for God the author and Creator of all substances has created them both, but to the dissimilar choices and desires of these angels themselves . . .. It is nothing less than a perversion of the nature of the angels if they do not adhere to God . . .. What makes the wicked angels differ from the good ones is not their nature but a perversion or imperfection.

Although no one can define the precise measure of their wisdom before the fall, one thing is certain. We cannot presume that they shared in wisdom equally with the angels who enjoy a plenitude of true happiness precisely because they were never deceived concerning its eternity.

. . . the rebel angels, by reason of their sin, have died in the sense that, in abandoning God, they gave up the fountain of life which had enabled them to live in wisdom and blessedness. However, they could not die in the sense of ceasing to live and to feel, since they, too, were created immortal. That is why, even when the final judgment hurls them into a second death, they will not be wholly dead, for they will never lack the sense of the pains they are to suffer. (AUGUSTINE)[175]

Satan has his command set up in the Second Heaven. He has a government, a ruling order, and a chain of command. Apart from the ruling order, there is also a social order. These two are related in that the ruling order comes from the top of the social order (Ephesians 1:21 and Ephesians 6:12). Even before my experience, I was aware of the Bible's teachings relative to this, but in no way did I imagine it to be as elaborate and profound as it really is.

Satan's social order is discriminatory. There is an established difference between orders of spirit beings in that world which allows some of the spirit beings to reside at a higher level of existence than others. The closest comparison to this order on the earth is the caste system of the nation of India. The caste system produces "untouchables" in the Second Heaven, just as it does on earth. I soon discovered there are no general practitioners in all of that demon world. Each demon is an expert. They have only one area of expertise, and they work this area very well.

As the escorting angel would point out the demons, each group was named. I saw them in all sizes and shapes. Some looked liked humans, some looked like giant humans, and some looked half-human and half animal. Some looked like known animals of the world, but some looked so horrible that it almost produced nausea to look upon them. I saw some in forms and shapes that the human mind cannot imagine. The Bible indicates these weird shapes and forms in Revelation 16:13.

The chain of command on each project was explained to me. On each project, the demon from the highest order is in command. The demon from the second ranking is next in line and so on down the order. This chain of command is always the way it works with possibly one exception. That exception would be a project, which involves what I call the "mystery" demon.

All demons working on a project know the chain of command and cannot bypass it. The demon in charge is the only one authorized to speak for the project . . .. Rarely, if ever, is a human being possessed by just one demon.

These were the five groups that were emphasized to me. Number one, of course, was the giant, warring demons. This group also ranks number one in order. In the number two group there are the demons of hate, lust, strife, and a few other demons; the primary member of this group is the demon of greed who is being used greatly in this last day attack. This group also ranks number two in order. The third group is the group that possesses skills in the area of the dark arts, such as witchcraft, false religion, self-destruction, fear, magic, sorcery, occult, ESP and related psychic phenomena, and others. Important as this group is the demon of necromancy (speaking with the dead). This group also ranks third in order.

The next group shown me was what I call the mystery demon group. I was not permitted to retain all that was shown me about this group of demons and I don't know why. They are the ones that are always involved when Satan wants to work in a person and has to ask special permission from God. These are also the ones used in children and must be handled in a different way. (Matthew 17:21) Over ninety per cent of all demon activity in humans is limited to those humans who are at or over the level of accountability. When demon activity is involved in those under the level of accountability, it is done so on a permission basis only. When this type of possession occurs, this mystery demon is the one involved. He has the ability to manifest himself in humans as epilepsy. I was not permitted to retain in my memory the shape or form of this demon and I cannot remember if they even told me his place of rank or order. One thing I do remember about him is that his power over flesh is far greater than the other demons because of his great anonymity.

The fifth group emphasized was the last in rank and order. The shapes and forms of these demons were so horrible to look upon that it almost produced nausea. They were in shapes and forms so despicable that the mind of man could not imagine them. They possessed skills in the areas of perversion . . .. These are the ones charged with the responsibility of lowering the morals of mankind. These demons appear to man as something beautiful and desirable, but I saw them for what they are, ugly and horrible. If all who practice perversion could but look upon these creatures who promote it, they could never enjoy that perversion again.

These five groups do NOT make up all the different groups of demons, but these were the groups emphasized to me. (PITTMAN)[176]

I like bats much better than bureaucrats. I am in the Managerial Age, in a world of "Admin." The greatest evil is not now done in those sordid "dens of crime" that Dickens loved to paint. It is not done even in concentration camps and labor camps. In those we see its final result. But it is conceived and ordered (moved, seconded, carried, and minuted [sic]) in clean, carpeted, warmed, and well-lighted offices, by quiet men with white collars and cut fingernails and smooth-shaven cheeks who do not need to raise their voice. Hence, naturally enough, my symbol for Hell is something like the bureaucracy of a police state or the offices of a thoroughly nasty business concern. (C. S. LEWIS)[177]

Are demons bound in hell?
Scriptures
4. Gen 6:1-4 - The Nephilim were on the earth in those days . . . the sons of God went to the daughters of men and had children by them. (NIV)

5. Matt 12:43-45 - When an evil spirit comes out of a man, it goes through arid places seeking rest and does not find it. Then it says, "I will return to the house I left." When it arrives, it finds the house unoccupied, swept clean and put in order. Then it goes and takes with it seven other spirits more wicked than itself, and they go in and live there. And the final condition of that man is worse than the first. (NIV)

6. Lk 8:31 - And they begged him repeatedly not to order them to go into the Abyss. (NIV)

7. 2 Pet 2:4 - . . . God did not spare angels when they sinned, but sent them to hell, putting them into gloomy dungeons to be held for judgment. (NIV)

8. Jude 6 - And the angels who did not keep their positions of authority but abandoned their own home—these he has kept in darkness, bound with everlasting chains for judgment on the great Day. (NIV)

Commentary
All demons were originally free demons, but some of these have been confined.

Some demons are confined temporarily after being cast out of a person [Lk 8:31] . . . and then later released. Many others are confined temporarily now to be released for specific judgments of the Great Tribulation.

The place where temporarily confined demons are confined is the Abyss.

The second category of confined demons are demons that have been confined permanently and will never be released, but who will move directly into the Lake of Fire. (FRUCHTENBAUM)[178]

Also note that the earth is the demon's place of habitation and not Hell; however, there are some demons already chained in Hell. These demons who are presently in Hell are not Satan's working demons. One day they will all occupy Hell, but that day is not yet. (Matthew 8:29) Satan and the demons know what Hell is and they don't want to go there.

As was previously stated, not all demons remain free to work for Satan. Some of them have been taken and put into chains and are locked up. These are referred to as the chained demons and according to the scripture, they shall be let loose for a specified time in the great tribulation period. These are the demons spoken of in Jude 6 and 2 Peter 2:4.

Satan and his demons are allowed to work within certain time limits and within certain bounds. Anytime they go beyond these bounds, they must have permission. (PITTMAN)[179]

Some scholars assert that the sin of the angels who were cast to Tartarus—referred to in II Peter 2:4 and Jude 6—was in being seduced to leave their own habitation (heaven) to satisfy their amorous desire for "strange flesh" (beings of another nature on earth). But, that angels are not endowed with the propensities for reproduction is clearly inferred in the fact that there is no marriage among the angels (Matthew 22:30), and marriage implies procreation. . . . To be capable of changing their nature, form and order to another order of created beings at will has no support in the Scriptures. Whatever the specific sin of angels, or whenever the imprisonment in Tartarus occurred, it makes little difference to the fact; some fallen angels, according to II Peter 2:4 and Jude 6, are already reserved (Greek test: "having been kept"), awaiting judgment that shall come upon all evil spirits, or *daimonia*. There is also a great host of demons free and active in Satan's kingdom, carrying out his evil will and purpose. (Ephesians 6:12). (EADE)[180]

The true meaning of the passage is that Moses designates as sons of God those people who had the promise of the blessed Seed. It is a term of the New Testament and designates the believers, who call God Father and whom God, in turn, calls sons. The Flood came, not because the Cainite race had become corrupt, but because the race of the righteous who had believed God, obeyed His Word, and observed true worship had fallen into idolatry, disobedience of parent, sensual pleasures, and the practice of oppression. (LUTHER)[181]

Personal account

Finally, my escorting angels brought me to a group of these odd-looking beings. They began to explain to me that this group was the "untouchables" of the Second Heaven, and it was the fifth group to be emphasized to me, so they ranked last in order of command . . .. This group of demons had the most despicable shapes and forms of any in all the Second Heaven. In many cases, the forms of some of them were so repulsive that just to look upon them produced nausea. Some of their forms were so odd that they defy description. Others were so small in stature that they were almost overlooked. I was astounded to learn that these were the creatures who held all the expertise in the area of "perversion". This group of untouchable, despicable, odd-looking spirit beings had been given the important assignment of destroying the morals of modern man. . . . the angels told me that I was going to be permitted to see a human being actually being possessed by one of these demons.

We entered the physical room . . . about three feet from those two people, being close enough to reach out and touch them. I could "hear" and understand each word they said, however, they could not see, hear, or feel me or the angels.

Standing between them was the most despicable looking of all creatures, of which they were totally unaware. He looked like an overgrown, stuffed, green frog that was all out of shape. The man and woman were talking and laughing as though they had just exchanged a joke. The demon, however, was between them and moving slowly toward the man's face. His every movement was calculated, much as a cat's movement is calculated when he is stalking a little bird. . . . I could not communicate to him because I was totally in the spirit.

When the demon reached the man's face, suddenly, like a puff of smoke, he disappeared into the man's face, appearing to have penetrated the pores of the skin. The angel said to me, "There, it is finished. He is possessed." . . . The angel stated that this individual, by his own sovereign will, had openly invited this thing to enter. To the man, the demon looked so desirable and beautiful, but I see him for what he truly is—ugly, despicable, and nauseating. I watched in amazement as the demons went about their business stalking their human victims. It was obvious that his stalking was not done on a random basis, but was a very personal thing with each person already having been targeted.

The next statement I would like to make is very critical and most important. In spite of all the preparation and temptation of these spirit beings, man does not have to yield! If he does so, it will be because he does so by his own sovereign will. (PITTMAN)[182]

Review of this lesson

How are demons referred to in the Bible? They are referred to as: Sons of God; familiar spirit, medium or spiritualist; to rule or to be lord; goat idols; evil spirit; lying spirit; angels of evil; destroys; idols; night creatures, night demons; Fortune, Destiny, Fate; to be controlled by a demon from within; evil power; demon; to be very reverent to demons; demon worship; demonical; Unclean spirit; evil spirit; wicked spirit; seducing spirit; spirit of demons; angels; *Abaddon, Apollyon*, destruction.

When did the demons fall and how many? One-third of the angels fell with Satan.

Are demons organized? They are probably organized and mirror the organization of angels.

Do demons reside in hell? Some of them do.

Preview of the next lesson

The next lesson will cover the activities of fallen angels.

Lesson 12 - WHAT ARE THE ACTIVITIES OF DEMONS?

The demons mimic the activities of their master, Satan. In the end, all will be defeated by Jesus as depicted in this painting by Goethe as published in Goethe's Works by George Barrie. (Some images © 2003-2004 www.clipart.com, #470924)

Review of the previous lesson

The names of fallen angels are: sons of God; familiar spirit, medium or spiritualist; to rule or to be lord; goat idols; evil spirit; lying spirit; angels of evil; destroys; idols; night creatures, night demons; Fortune, Destiny, Fate; to be controlled by a demon from within; evil power; demon; to be very reverent to demons; demon worship; demonical; Unclean spirit; evil spirit; wicked spirit; seducing spirit; spirit of demons; angels; *Abaddon, Apollyon,* destruction.

One third of the angels fell with Satan and are most probably organized.

Some of the fallen angels reside in Hell.

Preview of this lesson

What are some characteristics of demons?
Do demons attack the church?
Will Satan and his demons be defeated?

What are some characteristics of demons?

Scriptures

1. Matt 4:23-24 – . . . the demon-possessed . . . . (NIV) Matt 8:16

2. Matt 8:28-29 – . . . two demon-possessed men coming from the tombs met him. They were so violent that no one could pass that way. "What do you want with us, Son of God?" they shouted. "Have you come here to torture us before the appointed time?" (NIV)

3. Matt 12:22 – . . . a demon-possessed man who was blind and mute, and Jesus healed him, so that he could both talk and see. (NIV)

4. Mk 1:23-26 – . . . a man in their synagogue who was possessed by an evil spirit cried out, "What do you want with us, Jesus of Nazareth? Have you come to destroy us? I know who you are—the Holy One of God!" "Be quiet!" said Jesus sternly. "Come out of him!" The evil spirit shook the man violently and came out of him with a shriek. (NIV)

5. Mk 9:17-27 – A man in the crowd answered, "Teacher, I brought you my son, who is possessed by a spirit that has robbed him of speech. Whenever it seizes him, it throws him to the ground. He foams at the mouth, gnashes his teeth and becomes rigid." . . . When the spirit saw Jesus, it immediately threw the boy into a convulsion. He fell to the ground and rolled around, foaming at the mouth. Jesus asked the boy's father, "How long has he been like this?" "From childhood," he answered. "It has

often thrown him into fire or water to kill him. But if you can do anything, take pity on us and help us." (NIV)

6. Lk 8:27 – . . . demon-possessed man from the town. For a long time this man had not worn clothes or lived in a house, but had lived in the tombs. (NIV)

7. Mk 5:1-5 – . . . a man with an evil spirit came from the tombs to meet him. This man lived in the tombs, and no one could bind him any more, not even with a chain. For he had often been chained hand and foot, but he tore the chains apart and broke the irons on his feet. No one was strong enough to subdue him. Night and day among the tombs and in the hills he would cry out and cut himself with stones. (NIV)

8. Lk 13:10-11 – . . . a woman was there who had been crippled by a spirit for eighteen years. She was bent over and could not straighten up at all. (NIV)

9. Acts 8:7 – With shrieks, evil spirits came out of many, and many paralytics and cripples were healed.

10. Acts 16:16 – . . . a slave girl who had a spirit by which she predicted the future. (NIV)

11. Acts 19:15 – One day the evil spirit answered them, "Jesus I know, and I know about Paul, but who are you?" Then the man who had the evil spirit jumped on them and overpowered them all. He gave them such a beating that they ran out of the house naked and bleeding. (NIV)

12. Matt 12:43-45 – When an evil spirit comes out of a man, it goes through arid places seeking rest and does not find it. Then it says, "I will return to the house I left." When it arrives, it finds the house unoccupied, swept clean and put in order. Then it goes and takes with it seven other spirits more wicked than itself, and they go in and live there. And the final condition of that man is worse than the first. (NIV)

Commentary

When a man has lowered his sovereign will and allowed demons possession, then the good, invisible spirits known as God's angels cannot help him since man willfully allowed this possession. God's angels, who are here to help man, cannot violate man's will in the matter. When the possession becomes complete, as in the Biblical account in Mark 5, man is then a prisoner, unable to even ask for help. Remember, that the man in Mark was possessed because he allowed it. Even though these evil spirits lied to him, he was not forced to believe the lie. He made the choice to believe it. The rare exception to this type of demon possession is found in less than ten per cent of the cases, and then only by special permission from God. This type possession is allowed in special cases and for special purposes. (PITTMAN)[183]

First, they are spirit beings . . . they do not have physical bodies . . . they have clear shapes and features, which are frequently animal-like . . .

111

they seek to possess man, since to some extent their power is dependent upon their possession of men.

Second . . . is their power . . . they have power to control men from within . . . they can afflict men . . . demons can perform miracles . . . . And,

Third . . . they are, in their morality, unclean . . . they are corrupt to their nature . . . they are fierce and vicious . . . they are also vile and malicious . . . . they are characterized by extreme viciousness . . . they have a counterfeit system of doctrine . . . their immorality leads to more immorality . . . they are described as being part of this darkness controlled by Satan . . . they are not all equally wicked.

Fourthly, they have the ability to appear visibly. (FRUCHTENBAUM)[184]

Do demons attack the church?
Scriptures
13. Rom 15:21-22 – . . . I have often been hindered from coming to you. (NIV)

14. Eph 5:18 – Do not get drunk on wine, which leads to debauchery. (NIV)

15. Eph 6:12 – . . . our struggle is . . . against the rulers, against the authorities, against the powers of this dark world and against the spiritual forces of evil in the heavenly realms. (NIV)

16. 1 Tim 4:1-3 – . . . the time will come when men will not put up with sound doctrine. . . . they will gather around them a great number of teachers to say what their itching ears want to hear. (NIV)

Commentary
When the Devil saw the human race abandoning the temples of demons and marching happily forward in the name of the freedom-giving Mediator, he inspired heretics to oppose Christian teaching under cover of the Christian name as though their presence in the City of God could go unchallenged . . . .

Heretics are those who entertain in Christ's Church unsound and distorted ideas and stubbornly refuse, even when warned, to return to what is sound and right, to correct their contagious and death-dealing doctrines, but go on defending them. (AUGUSTINE)[185]

Demonic control involves a demon residing in a person and exercising direct control over that person with a certain degree of derangement of the mind and/or physical upset of the body.

Demonic harassment where a demon harasses a person and the harassment comes from without.

Demonic influence . . . Peter had been influenced by Satan to try to dissuade Jesus from going to the cross . . .. Demonic harassment and demonic influence are activities outside the person, but demonic control takes place inside the person.

In light of this definition, can a demon control a Christian: . . . A believer can never be possessed by a demon in the sense of ownership. . . . Can a believer be controlled by a demon from within? the answer is: Yes, he can. The Holy Spirit controls from within and so, then, must Satan, since the same Greek word is used.

The distinction between believers and unbelievers . . . is a matter of the extent of control. An unbeliever can be totally controlled, but a believer can only be partially controlled.

How can a demon reside in the same body with the Holy Spirit? Most believers admit that they still have a sin-nature. The Holy Spirit coexists with the sin-nature of the believer . . .. The Holy Spirit resides in the new nature, not in the old sin-nature. The demon resides not in the new nature, but in the old sin-nature. The fact that there are two natures coexisting within the believer shows why both a demon and the Holy Spirit can coexist within the believer: They reside in two different natures.

Demonic control can be repeated.

How can one tell if someone is or is not controlled by a demon from within? . . . symptoms of demonic control by and of themselves do not prove that demons are residing in the person, because there may be other problems that cause these same symptoms. Because a person has one or more of these symptoms is not definite evidence that person has a demon within him . . . physical disease . . . mental derangement . . . deep depression . . . self reproach . . . suicide . . . passivity . . . immorality . . . bitterness . . . drug abuse . . . psychic power . . . animal-like tendencies . . . restlessness during Bible reading . . . multiple personalities .

What causes some people to have a demon residing in them? . . . inheritance . . . experimentation . . . transference by contact with the occult . . . unconfessed sin.

What are the cures for demonic control? . . . receiving Christ . . . confession of sin . . . renunciation. This involves those who have fallen under demonic control by inheritance . . . removal of all occult objects . . . resist the devil so that he will flee away.

The ultimate cure for demonic control is exorcism . . . clearly taught in Scripture . . . in the name of Jesus Christ . . . by the power of the Holy Spirit . . . with a simple word, that is, with a command . . . that word is, Get out in the name of Jesus Christ. Fourthly, it must be done by faith . . .. Fifthly, there are certain types of demons that cannot simply be ordered out . . . some demons can only be forced out by using the authority in the name of Christ.

The believer can force the demon out himself. That is why, in dealing with Satan, the believer is encouraged to do one thing: to resist. (FRUCHTENBAUM)[186]

Will Satan be defeated?
Scriptures

17. Gen 3:15 – . . . I will put enmity between you and the woman, and between your offspring and hers; he will crush your head, and you will strike his heel. (NIV)

18. Matt 25:41 – . . . he will say to those on his left, Depart from me, you who are cursed, into the eternal fire prepared for the devil and his angels. (NIV)

19. Rev 20:10 – . . . the devil, who deceived them, was thrown into the lake of burning sulfur, where the beast and the false prophet had been thrown. They will be tormented day and night forever and ever. (NIV)

Commentary

God foresaw the defeat, which the Devil would suffer at the hands of a descendant of Adam, and with the help of divine grace, and that this would be to the greater glory of the saints. (AUGUSTINE)[187]

[Gen 3:15] This amounts to saying: You, Satan, have attacked and deceived man through the woman that through sin you might pose as their head and lord. I, in turn, shall lie in wait with the very same weapon. I will take the woman and raise up a Descendant from her, and the Descendant will crush your head. Through sin you have corrupted and made guilty of death the nature of mankind; but out of this very flesh I will produce such a Man as shall crush and lay low both you and all your powers.

So the devil is angry because God intends to tread him underfoot through flesh and blood. If a great spirit were his opponent, he would not be so angry. (LUTHER)[188]

The first judgment of Satan was the judgment when he first sinned at the time of his fall (Ezekiel 28:16).

His second judgment came in Eden as a result of his temptation of Adam and Eve.

The third judgment of Satan was at the cross. Satan suffered a specific judgment at the time that Christ died. Satan knew it was coming, and that is why he tried to do everything he could to keep Christ from the cross.

These first judgments upon Satan are all history; but there are four more judgments yet to come.

Fourthly, in the middle of the Tribulation, Satan will be cast out of his present third abode and cast into his fourth abode, the earth. He will be confined to the earth for the second half of the Tribulation (Revelation 12:

114

7-9) so that he will no longer have any access into heaven (Revelation 12: 10-12a).

Fifthly, he will be judged by being imprisoned in the abyss during the Millennium. Sixthly, at the Great White Throne Judgment, Satan will be judged by the church.

Seventhly, his final judgment will be the Lake of Fire. (FRUCHTENBAUM)[189]

Personal account

Michael said, "Up until the appointed time, our task is not to destroy Satan, but to scatter the forces of darkness, to hold them in abeyance, to overcome them and to keep them from God's people."

Then he said, "I have an assignment that I am anxiously awaiting where I am not going to have to show respect for Lucifer any more. That assignment is to sweep the heavens clean of Satan and every single one of his angels. We will not leave even one!" (BUCK)[190]

Review of this lesson

Do demons attack the church? Demons may manifest in demon control from within, harassment, hindering, deception.

What are some characteristics of demons? They are unclean, sullen, violent, malicious, powerful, spirits, limited knowledge.

Will Satan and his demons be defeated? Yes. They are already defeated by the cross.

Review lessons 8-12

Lesson 8 – Who is Satan?

Lesson 9 – What about Satan's fall?

Lesson 10 – How does Satan interact with mankind?

Lesson 11 – Who are the fallen angels?

Lesson 12 – What are the activities of demons?

Preview of the next lesson

The next lesson discusses possible references to Jesus in the Old Testament.

Mark R. Erickson

Lesson 13 - AN ANGEL OF SPECIAL STATUS

Did Jesus visit the earth in the Old Testament? You decide. This is not really a depiction of Jesus in the Old Testament. But, I had to get one more picture of Jesus in here. This is a picture of Jesus with disciples as published by James Sangster & Company in Pilgrim's Progress (The Illustrated Family Bunyan) (Some images © 2003-2004 www. clipart.com, #55756).

Review of the previous five lessons

Lesson 8 – Who is Satan?

Lesson 9 – What about Satan's fall?

Lesson 10 – How does Satan interact with mankind?

Lesson 11 – Who are the fallen angels?

Lesson 12 – What are the activities of demons?

Possible references to Jesus in the Old Testament:

Note:

There are many references to angels in the Old Testament. Many references also indicate there was an angel with a special position with God. A few of these scriptures are given in this lesson. Maybe this angel was Jesus? This topic is definitely wide open for discussion and there is some disagreement. Let the Holy Spirit guide you through this material. If nothing else, you may have learned a new word – theophany. Commentaries are scarce on this topic.

Did Jesus appear in the Old Testament?

Scriptures

The Angel

(This term is used only 2 times by itself. Other times it is used in association with other more descriptive terms like "the angel of the Lord." It is used in association with other terms in Gen 16, Zech, 1 Chr 21, and 2 Sam 24.)

1. Gen 48:15,16 – Then . . . Joseph and said, "May the God before whom my fathers Abraham and Isaac walked, the God who has been my shepherd all my life to this day, the Angel who has delivered me from all harm . . . . (NIV)

2. Hos 12:4-5 – He struggled with the angel and overcame him; he wept and begged for his favor. He found him at Bethel and talked with him there - the LORD God Almighty, the LORD is his name of renown! (NIV)

The Angel of the Lord

(This term is used 54 times in the Old Testament. A few examples are given below.)

3. Gen 16:9-11 – Then the angel of the LORD told her, "Go back to your mistress and submit to her." The angel added, "I will so increase your descendants that they will be too numerous to count." The angel of the LORD also said to her: "You are now with child and you will have a son. You shall name him Ishmael, for the LORD has heard of your misery." (NIV)

4. Gen 22:11-19 – But the angel of the LORD called out to him from heaven, Abraham! Abraham! (NIV)

5. Ex 3:2-6 – There the angel of the LORD appeared to him in flames of fire from within a bush. . . . When the LORD saw that he had gone over to look, God called to him from within the bush, "Moses! Moses! . . . Do not come any closer," God said. "Take off your sandals, for the place where you are standing is holy ground." Then he said, "I am the God of your father, the God of Abraham, the God of Isaac and the God of Jacob." At this, Moses hid his face, because he was afraid to look at God. (NIV).

6. Judg 2:1-5 – The angel of the LORD went up from Gilgal to Bokim and said, "I brought you up out of Egypt and led you into the land that I swore to give to your forefathers. I said, I will never break my covenant with you, and you shall not make a covenant with the people of this land, but you shall break down their altars. Yet you have disobeyed me. Why have you done this? Now therefore I tell you that I will not drive them out before you; they will be [thorns] in your sides and their gods will be a snare to you." When the angel of the LORD had spoken these things to all the Israelites, the people wept aloud, and they called that place Bokim. There they offered sacrifices to the LORD. (NIV)

7. Judg 6:11-18 – The angel of the LORD came and sat down under the oak . . . the angel of the LORD appeared to Gideon, he said, "The LORD is with you, mighty warrior." . . . The LORD turned to him and said, "Go in the strength you have and save Israel out of Midian's hand. Am I not sending you?". . . The LORD answered, "I will be with you, and you will strike down all the Midianites together." . . . And the LORD said, I will wait until you return. (NIV)

8. Judg 13:17-19 – Then Manoah inquired of the angel of the LORD, "What is your name, so that we may honor you when your word comes true?" He replied, "Why do you ask my name? It is beyond understanding." (NIV)

9. 2 Sam 24:16 – When the angel stretched out his hand to destroy Jerusalem, the LORD was grieved because of the calamity and said to the angel who was afflicting the people, Enough! Withdraw your hand. The angel of the LORD was then at the threshing floor of Araunah the Jebusite. (NIV)

10. Zech 3:1-2 - Then he showed me Joshua the high priest standing before the angel of the LORD, and Satan standing at his right side to accuse him. (NIV)

The Angel of God

(This term is used only 5 times in the Old Testament.)

11. Gen 21:17-21 – God heard the boy crying, and the angel of God called to Hagar from heaven . . .. God opened her eyes and she saw a well of water . . . God was with the boy as he grew up. (NIV)

12. Gen 31:11-13 – The angel of God said to me in the dream, "Jacob." I answered, "Here I am." . . . I am the God of Bethel, where you anointed a pillar and where you made a vow to me. . . .

13. Ex 14:19-20 – Then the angel of God, who had been traveling in front of Israel's army, withdrew and went behind them. The pillar of cloud also moved from in front and stood behind them . . .. (NIV)

14. Judg 6:20-21 - The angel of God said to him, Take the meat and the unleavened bread, place them on this rock, and pour out the broth. And Gideon did so. (NIV)

15. Judg 13:9-21 – God heard Manoah, and the angel of God came again to the woman while she was out in the field . . .. The angel of the LORD answered, Your wife must do all that I have told her. . . . The angel of the LORD replied, "Even though you detain me, I will not eat any of your food. But if you prepare a burnt offering, offer it to the LORD." (Manoah did not realize that it was the angel of the LORD.) Then Manoah inquired of the angel of the LORD, "What is your name, so that we may honor you when your word comes true?" He replied, "Why do you ask my name? It is beyond understanding." Then Manoah took a young goat, together with the grain offering, and sacrificed it on a rock to the LORD. And the LORD did an amazing thing while Manoah and his wife watched: As the flame blazed up from the altar toward heaven, the angel of the LORD ascended in the flame. Seeing this, Manoah and his wife fell with their faces to the ground. When the angel of the LORD did not show himself again to Manoah and his wife, Manoah realized that it was the angel of the LORD. (NIV)

The Angel of His Presence

(This term is used only 1 time in the Old Testament.)

16. Isa 63:9 – In all their distress he too was distressed, and the angel of his presence saved them. In his love and mercy he redeemed them; he lifted them up and carried them all the days of old. (NIV)

His Angel

(This term is used only 4 times in the Old Testament.)

17. Gen 24:7-8 - The LORD . . . who spoke to me and promised me on oath, saying, "To your offspring I will give this land." . . . he will send his angel before you so that you can get a wife for my son from there. (NIV)

18. Gen 24:40-41 - He replied, "The LORD, before whom I have walked, will send his angel with you and make your journey a success . . .." (NIV)

19. Dan 3:28 – Then Nebuchadnezzar said, "Praise be to the God of Shadrach, Meshach and Abednego, who has sent his angel and rescued his servants!" (NIV)

20. Dan 6:21-22 – Daniel answered . . . "My God sent his angel, and he shut the mouths of the lions." (NIV)

My Angel

(This term is used only 2 times in the Old Testament.)

21. Ex 23:20-23 - See, I am sending an angel ahead of you to guard you along the way and to bring you to the place I have prepared. . . . listen to what he says. Do not rebel against him; he will not forgive your rebellion, since my Name is in him. . . . listen carefully to what he says and do all that I say, I will be an enemy to your enemies and will oppose those who oppose you. My angel will go ahead of you and bring you into the land of the Amorites, Hittites, Perizzites, Canaanites, Hivites and Jebusites, and I will wipe them out. (NIV)

22. Ex 32:34 – Now go, lead the people to the place I spoke of, and my angel will go before you. (NIV)

The Lord – three men

23. Gen 18 – The Lord appeared to Abraham . . . Abraham looked up and saw three men . . . "Have I found favor in your eyes Lord"? . . . Then the Lord said, . . .

The One

24. Gen 16:13 - Gen 16:13 . . . she [Hagar] said, "I have now seen the One who sees me." . . . (NIV)

Melchizedek

25. Gen 14:18 - Then Melchizedek king of Salem brought out bread and wine. He was priest of God Most High, ... Then Abram gave him a tenth of everything. (NIV)

Commentary

How are we to understand *theophanies*? (This is a theological term for the visible appearances of Jesus Christ in other forms prior to His incarnation.) Some of the passages in the Old Testament tell us that the second person of the Trinity appeared and was called either "the Lord" or "the angel of the Lord." Nowhere is it clearer than in Genesis 18:9 where three men appear before Abraham.

We must remember, then, that in some cases in the Old Testament God Himself appeared in human form as an angel. This reinforces the idea of the relationship between God and His angels. Nevertheless, in almost

121

all of the cases where angelic personages appear they are God's created angelic beings and not God Himself. (GRAHAM)[191]

A study of these passages shows that while the angel and Yahweh are at times distinguished from each other, they are with equal frequency, and in the same passages, merged into each other. How is this to be explained? It is obvious that these apparitions cannot be the Almighty Himself, whom no man hath seen, or can see. In seeking the explanation, special attention should be paid to two of the passages above cited. In Ex 23:20 God promises to send an angel before His people to lead them to the promised land; they are commanded to obey him and not to provoke him for he will not pardon your transgression: for my name is in him. Thus the angel can forgive sin, which only God can do, because of God's name. His character and thus His authority, are in the angel. Further, in the passage Ex 32:34-33:17 Moses intercedes for the people after their first breach of the covenant; God responds by promising, "Behold mine angel shall go before thee;" and immediately after God says, I will not go up in the midst of thee. In answer to further pleading, God says, "My presence shall go with thee, and I will give thee rest." Here a clear distinction is made between an ordinary angel, and the angel who carries with him God's presence. The conclusion may be summed up in the words of Davidson in his Old Testament Theology: "In particular providences one may trace the presence of Yahweh in influence and operation; in ordinary angelic appearances one may discover Yahweh present on some side of His being, in some attribute of His character; in the angel of the Lord He is fully present as the covenant God of His people, to redeem them." The question still remains, who is the *theophanic* angel? To this many answers have been given, of which the following may be mentioned:

(1) This angel is simply an angel with a special commission; (2) He may be a momentary descent of God into visibility; (3) He may be the Logos, a kind of temporary pre-incarnation of the second person of the Trinity. Each has its difficulties, but the last is certainly the most tempting to the mind. Yet it must be remembered that at best these are only conjectures that touch on a great mystery. It is certain that from the beginning God used angels in human form, with human voices, in order to communicate with man; and the appearances of the angel of the Lord, with his special redemptive relation to God's people, show the working of that Divine mode of self-revelation which culminated in the coming of the Savior, and are thus a fore-shadowing of, and a preparation for, the full revelation of God in Jesus Christ. Further than this, it is not safe to go. (ORR)[192]

Many Christian writers have thought that this [Melchisedec] was an appearance of the Son of God himself, our Lord Jesus, known to Abram, at this time, by this name, as afterwards, Hagar called him by another name, Gen 16:13. (HENRY)[193]

Personal account

I was thrilled when a Christian brother, John Weaver, told me about how he was visited twice by an angel.

I was fixing my car alongside the road, I saw a car coming right across the plowed field about a quarter of a mile from me. It was a brand new car and the dirt and dust were flying behind it as it came right across a plowed field at me. He drove me into town so I could secure help and then instantly disappeared. I learned later that it was an angel coming to my rescue. God visited me in a very special way again in 1971 and spoke to me about the work I was to do for Him. At this point in time in my ministry and my spiritual development, God in His grace saw fit to send the same angel to speak to me once again who had helped me approximately twenty years earlier. It was wintertime in Montana and some friends and I went hunting for elk . . . I was two-thirds of the way to the top of the ridge where I was headed when I saw a man coming out of the trees on the next ridge near the timberline. He did not have on Hunter orange and was walking right down to me without carrying a gun. He seemed to be walking at the same pace a normal man would walk, but he covered the ground between us so quickly . . . in a matter of seconds! I noticed that as he walked, HE LEFT NO FOOTPRINTS IN THE SNOW!

The man walked up to me and shook my hand. He said "John, do you know who I am?" I responded, speaking out of my spirit, "Yes, you are a servant of the Lord." He said, "Yes, that is right. The Lord has sent me here today to talk with you." We sat down on two big rocks facing each other. It was not until later that I realized I was talking with the same angel who had helped me when my car broke town twenty years earlier!

We talked about how God was pleased that I had moved my prayer life from a selfish prayer to one of compassion for those around me, and among other things, about needing a house for my family . . . at that point the angel stopped me! This was the first time he had said anything since I had begun sharing with him. He said, "How much money do you need?" I said, "Maybe $20,000.

The angel said, "You know that I could give you that $20,000 in hundred dollar bills right now, don't you?" Somehow I knew he could do it, so I replied, "Yes." He said, "We don't do things that way, though. The Lord puts it upon the hearts of His people. That money will be taken care of and you don't have to tell anyone. It will just come in." He talked with me twenty or thirty minutes more, telling me some beautiful truths and some exciting things about how it would be in eternity in heaven. What a thrill!

I was amazed at what the angel had said, but I became more amazed as he began to share some principles that were to change my life. The angel said, "John, you have a ministry that is eternal. It is not just earthly, it is eternal! the little things that you are doing now, your ministry and your faithfulness now, are going to determine your destiny of tomorrow, your ministry of tomorrow. To the degree that you will humble yourself and minister under His direction, you will be just what God wants you to be."

Another thing he said was, "God has given you alternatives and allowed you to make choices. You can choose to be close to Him and be used by Him or you can go your own way, do your own thing and live a selfish life. What you do here and the choices you make here will all be reflected in your relationship with God when you get to heaven. You will realize that there are not just crowns put on your head, but there will be rewards of relationship and ministry being given to you also. If you will be faithful here, God will give you an increased ministry there."

Two weeks later, I was driving back from a meeting, worshipping the Lord in the car and thinking about the $20,000 the angel had mentioned. Suddenly, I felt the Lord's presence in the car right beside me. Whether it was the angel again speaking for the Lord, or the Lord speaking directly I do no know. He spoke to me about the $20,000, reminding me that I had never asked for it. When I replied by asking, He said, "Starting tomorrow morning, that money is going to come in." And just like that, it was as though he slipped out of the moving car and was gone!

God loves us enough that He has prepared everything that we need for our deliverance and our help. He has sent His Holy Spirit to be with us, to teach us, and watch over us. The angels encamp around us! How can we lose? Angels are on assignment today! Hallelujah! (BUCK)[194]

Review of this lesson

Jesus very possibly appeared to selected people in the Old Testament.

Review of this study

Lesson 1 - Introduction

Lesson 2 – Who Are Holy Angels?

Lesson 3 – What are the traits of holy angels?

Lesson 4 – How do holy angels interact with humans?

Lesson 5 – Functions of holy angels with humans?

Lesson 6 – Organization of holy angels?

Lesson 7 – Functions of holy angels with God?

Lesson 8 – Who is Satan?

Lesson 9 – What about Satan's fall?

Lesson 10 – How does Satan interact with mankind?

Lesson 11 – Who are the fallen angels?

Lesson 12 – What are the activities of demons?

Lesson 13 – An angel of special status?

Angels are real. The Bible says so. Jesus says so. So are Satan and his demons. We are surrounded by a world unseen, a world of spiritual creatures, a world of heavenly creatures. Some are here to bring us harm, but most are here to protect, comfort, and help us. They are organized and numerous. Most of the time they go unseen, or at least unrecognized, but often do interact with us in visible and physical and very real ways. It should be comforting to us that God has laid out such an elaborate structure for his most precious of creation, humans. It is hard to believe that even though they are above us now, that some day we will be above them. It is hard to believe that they could learn anything from us. It is hard to believe that some could intentionally rebel against God and forever lose their position of glory. But, God has it all in control. It is interesting to note that just about every culture and every religion has some concept of angels. You can find sources that will list the names of thousands of angels. There are many books on angels. However, the purpose of this book was to restrict the study of angels to references made in the Bible. In addition, the purpose of this study was to provide a convenient reference for Bible study that could be used in any Bible class.

Commentary was provided only as an interesting sideline to give examples of what some authorities say about this topic. The intent of the commentary was to provide a diverse list of sources from various times in history to bring insights to the existence and study of angels. You will not agree with every comment, and you shouldn't, if you are a truly thinking Christian. But, I personally found the commentary very enlightening and encouraging. I hope it did the same for you. Take some time to review the Table of Contents to refresh in your mind the study of *Angels: The Good, The Bad and The Ugly.*

Visit me some time on the internet at angelstudy.com.

Remember, we are not to seek angels.

Seek Jesus!!!

INDEX

R

S

BIBLIOGRAPHY[a]

A Short Explanation of Dr. Martin Luther's Small Catechism, A Handbook of Christian Doctrine. Saint Louis: Concordia Publishing House, 1943. (Used by permission of Concordia Publishing House.)
Luther's Small Catechism was a question and answer text intended to be used by parents in instructing their children. Some of the material in this catechism is no longer found in the current catechism.

Augustine. *City of God.* (Gerald G. Walsh, Demetrius B. Zema, Grace, Monahan, and Daniel J. Honan, Trans.) Garden City: Image Books 1958. (Used by permission of The Catholic University of America Press.)
St. Augustine was the Bishop of Hippo in North Africa (395 AD). The City of God was one 118 works that he authored taking 14 years to complete. It was written on the request of a Roman official, a Christian, to fend off the persistent rumor that Christianity was to blame for Rome's decline in power. His works have been widely respected for centuries.

Bainton, Roland H. *The Martin Luther Christmas Book.* Philadelphia. Fortress Press, Philadelphia, 1963. (Used by permission of Augsburg Fortress Publishing House)
This book contains seven separate commentaries by Martin Luther on different topics of Christmas.
Black, Matthew. The Strange Vision of Enoch. Bible Review (Summer 1987), pp. 20-37.

Burnham, Sophy. *A Book of Angels.* New York. Ballantine Books, 1990. (Used by Permission of Ballantine Books.)

Her biography states in part that she is a writer and healer, and participates in services at the National Cathedral. Winner of several awards, she has written in a wide variety of styles: novels, plays, film-work, radio, political speeches, articles, essays, and some investigative journalism. This book contains a significant amount of research on the angelology of several religions in addition to Christianity. In addition, it contains letters written to her by individuals that had personal encounters with angelic beings. It is also a good resource book for angel art. It is not a Bible based study on angels.

Burnham, Sophy. *Angel Letters.* New York. Ballantine Books, 1991. (Used by Permission of Ballantine Books.)

In her Introduction, she states that, This book, the sequel to A Book of Angels, consists of a small selection of the many letters written in response to that earlier work. In fact, this book is predominantly personal accounts of encounters with angelic beings.

Brokering, Herbert F. *Luther's Prayers.* Minneapolis: Augsburg Publishing House, 1967. (Used by permission by Augsburg Fortress.)

Christenson, Evelyn. *Battling the Prince of Darkness, Rescuing Captives from Satan's Kingdom.* Wheaton, Illinois. Victor Books, 1990. (Used by permissions of Victor Books.)

Evelyn Christenson is also the author of *What Happens When Women Pray, Lord, Change Me!, and Gaining Through Losing.* She also conducts seminars and is a conference speaker. She is chairman of the United Prayer Ministries, St. Paul, Minnesota.

Davidson, Gustave. *A Dictionary of Angels, Including the Fallen Angels.* New York. The Free Press, 1967. (Used by permission by The Free Press)

Gustave Davidson was the author-editor of a dozen books in drama, biography, poetry and angelology, serving as consultant in the last-named field to Stueben Glass and The Kennedy Foundation. He began collecting angels as a hobby, and ended up being an expert on angels. His resources began with the Bible, but soon expanded his research beyond the Bible to every conceivable resource imaginable." This book is a vast dictionary resource of every conceivable angel, named or otherwise. It is a massive research document. However, much of the information is not Bible based.

Eade, Alfred Thompson, S. T. D. *The Panorama Bible Study, Course No. 2, The Study of Angelology*. Old Tappan. Fleming H. Revell Company, 1962. (Used by permission of Baker Books)
    One of a series of four panoramic studies. The author's approach to theology is dispensational. This study provides a unique visual approach with a series of panorama charts depicting Angelology and Satanology.

Fruchtenbaum, Arnold G., D. D. "Angelology: The Doctrine of the Elect Angels." Ariel Ministries, Tustin, CA, 1984, Manuscript Number 73. (Used by permission of Ariel Ministries.)
    Arnold Fruchtenbaum is a Bible teacher, radio Bible teacher, theologian, and founder of Ariel Ministries whose primary outreach is to the Jews. He is a Jew and a Christian. (He calls himself a "completed Jew.") He graduated from Dallas Theological Seminary. His commentary is always succinct, thorough, and enlightening.

Fruchtenbaum, Arnold G., Th.M, Ph.D. "Demonology: The Doctrine of Fallen Angels." Ariel Ministries, Tustin, CA, 1984, Manuscript Numbers 82. (Used by permission of Ariel Ministries.)

Fruchtenbaum, Arnold G., Th.M, Ph.D. "Santanology: The Doctrine of Satan." Ariel Ministries, Tustin, CA, 1984, Manuscript Number 77. (Used by permission of Ariel Ministries.)

Fruchtenbaum, Arnold G., Th.M, Ph.D. "The Fall of Satan According to Ezekiel 28:11-19." Ariel Ministries, Tustin, CA, 1984, Manuscript Number 156. (Used by permission of Ariel Ministries.)

Fruchtenbaum, Arnold G., Th.M, Ph.D. "The Six Abodes of Satan." Ariel Ministries, Tustin, CA, 1984, Manuscript Number 1. (Used by permission of Ariel Ministries.)

Graham, Billy. *Angel: God's Secret Agents.* Dallas: Word Publishing, 1975. (Used by permissions of Word Publishing.)
Billy Graham is respected over the world for his work, and inspired messages.

Henry, Matthew. *Matthew Henry's Commentary on the Whole Bible.* McLean. McDonald Publishing Company, six volumes. (Public Domain)
Matthew Henry is one of the mostly widely accepted and widely used Bible commentators for centuries. His original works were completed around 1702.

Hunter, Charles & Frances. *Angels on Assignment.* As told by Roland H. Buck. Kingwood: Hunter Books, 1979. (Used by permission of Charles and Francis Hunter.)
This book was published by the Hunters, based on an account related to them by Roland Buck concerning 18 visits he received from Gabriel and another angel named Chrioni. Roland Buck was an Assembly of God pastor for many years.

Jacobs, Henry Eyster. *A Summary of the Christian Faith.* Philadelphia: The United Lutheran Publication House, 1954.

Kepler, Thomas S., Editor. *The Table Talk of Martin Luther.* Grand Rapids: Baker Book House, 1952. (Public Domain)
A collection of quotations from Martin Luther based on his conversations/discussions with close associates. Traditionally, these discussions usually took place around the dinner table, hence the name of the book.

Lewis, C. S. *The Screwtape Letters.* New York: MacMillan Co, 1982. (Used by permission of MacMillan Co.)
C. S. Lewis was a professor of Medieval and Renaissance literature at Cambridge University circa World War II. This book is a fictional account of Satan's activities in the church.

Orr, James, General Editor. New International Version, International Bible Society, trans. sponsor. Colorado Springs, 1983.. *The International Standard Bible Encyclopaedia.* 12 Volumes. Grand Rapids: William B Eerdmans Publishing Co, 1952. (Used by permission of Eerdmans Publishing Co.)
   Originally published in 1915.

Pittman, Howard O. *Demons, An Eyewitness Account.* (No copyright).
   Howard Pittman was a Baptist minister for 35 years during which time he was also in law enforcement for 25 years. In 1979 he had a near death experience in which he was permitted to plea for a life extension before God. He was also given a tour through Satan's domain, what he calls the Second Heaven, by angels. First and foremost ,he places salvation in Jesus Christ.

Pittman, Howard O. *Placebo.* (No copyright).

Plass, Ewals M., Compiler. *What Luther Says.* 3 Volumes. Saint Louis: Concordia Publishing House, 1965. (used by permission of Concordia Publishing House.)
   This is an encyclopedic resource book of Martin Luther's comments covering almost every conceivable topic.

Tappert, Theodore G., Editor. *The Book of Concord.* Philadelphia: Fortress Press, 1959. (Used by permission of Augsburg Fortress.)
   The Book of Concord, or Book of Agreement, is a collection of Bible exposition and statements of faith, containing: three creeds, *"The Augsburg Confession" (1530), "Apology of the Augsburg Confession" (1531), "The Smalcald Articles" (1537), "Treatise on the Power and Primacy of the Pope" (1537), "The Small Catechism" (1529), "The Large Catechism" (1529), and "Formula of Concord" (1577).* It contains the writings of primarily Martin Luther and Philip Melanchthon. It is a cornerstone for Lutheran theology today as well as a history of the catalytic theology fueling the Reformation.

ENDNOTES

(Endnotes)

[1] Charles and Frances Hunter, *Angels on Assignment* (Kingwood, 1979), p. 16.

[2] Henry Eyster Jacobs, *A Summary of the Christian Faith* (Philadelphia, 1954), p 81.

[3] Thomas S. Kepler, *The Table Talk of Martin Luther* (Grand Rapids, 1952), #404.

[4] Hunter, *Angels on Assignment* (Kingwood, 1979),p. 48.

[5] Brokering, Luther's Prayers (Minneapolis, 1967) #182.

[6] Tappert., *The Book of Concord* (Philadelphis, 1959)p. 353.

[7] *Ibid.*

[8] 8Ewals Plass, *What Luther Says* (Saint Louis, 1965), Vol 1, p. 23, #61.

[9] Sophy Burnham, *Angel Letters* (New York, 1991), p. 31.

[10] Sophy Burnham, *A Book of Angels* (New York, 1990), p. 82.

[11] Arnold Fruchtenbaum, "Angelology: The Doctrine of the Elect Angels," Ariel Ministries, Manuscript Number 13, p. 1.

[12] *A Short Explanation of Dr. Martin Luther's Small Catechism, a Handbook of Christian Doctrine* (Saint Louis, 1943), pp. 93-94.

[13] Fruchtenbaum, Angelology . . . , pp. 1-2.

[14] Howard O. Pittman, *Demons, An Eyewitness Account*, p. 3.

[15] Billy Graham, *Angels: God's Secret Agents* (Dallas, 1975), p. 24, 30.

[16] Burnham, *A Book . . .* , p. 45

[17] Kepler, #404.

[18] Augustine, *The City of God (Garden City, 1958)* pp. 212-213, 215-217, 225-226.

[19] Matthew Henry, *Matthew Henry's Commentary on the Whole Bible*, Vol I, p. 2.

[20] Graham, p. 27.

[21] Burnham, A Book . . . , p. 82-83, 133.

[22] Fruchtenbaum, Angelology, p. 4.

[23] Graham, p. 27

[24] Hunter, p. 55.

[25] Pittman, p. 3.

[26] Roland H. Bainton, *The Martin Luther Christmas Book* (Philadelphia, 1980), p.45.

[27] Fruchtenbaum, *Angelology . . .* , p. 6.

[28] Jacobs, p. 80

[29] Fruchtenbaum, *Angelology . . .* , p. 3.

[30] Graham, p. 36, 41.

[31] Augustine, p. 294.

[32] Jacobs, p. 82.

[33] Fruchtenbaum, *Angelology . . .* , p. 7.

[34] Graham, p. 39

[35] Augustine, p. 222.

[36] Graham, p. 16.

[37] Augustine, p. 182.

[38] *Ibid.*, p. 240.

[39] Plass, Vol I, p. 25, # 68.

[40] Fruchtenbaum, *Angelology . . . , pp. 5-6.*

[41] Graham, p. 43.

[42] Jacob, p. 83..

[43] Graham, p. 43.

[44] Fruchtenbaum, *Angelology . . .* , p. 6.

[45] Pittman, p. 21.

[46] Graham, p. 45.

[47] Graham, p. 36.

[48] Fruchtenbaum, *Angelology . . .* , p. 7.

[49] Burnham, *A Book . . .* , p. 82-83, 133

[50] Burnham, *A Book . . .* , p. 45.

[51] Fruchtenbaum, *Angelology . . .* , p. 6.

[52] Graham, p. 40.

[53] Fruchtenbaum, *Angelology . . .* , p. 6.

[54] Graham, p. 26.

[55] Augustine, pp. 263, 533.

[56] Henry, Vol VI, p. 662.

[57] Graham., pp. 35-36.

[58] Fruchtenbaum, *Angelology . . .* , p. 5.

[59] Jacobs, p. 81.

[60] Hunter, p. 177.

[61] Plass, p. 25, #69.

[62] Pittman, p. 88.

[63] Burnham, *Angel Letters*, p. 86.

[64] Lewis, p. ix.

[65] Pittman, p. 4

[66] Bainton, pp. 44,46.

[67] Burnham, *A Book . . .* , pp. 110-111

[68] Graham, p. 42.

[69] Hunter, p. 42.

[70] Kepler, p. 279-280, #405.

[71] Plass, pp. 24-25, #64, #65, #67.

[72] Fruchtenbaum, *Angelology . . .* , p. 16.

[73] Jacob, pp. 83-83.

[74] Graham, p. 59, 73-74.

[75] Pittman, p. 59.

[76] Hunter, p. 40, 47.

[77] Kepler, p. 279, #404.

[78] Graham, pp. 43, 78-79.

[79] Plass, p. 26, #70, #71.

[80] Pittman, p. 59.

[81] Graham, pp. 88, 117

[82] Ibid., p. 76.

[83] Fruchtenbaum, *Angelology* . . . , p. 17.

[84] Augustine, p. 208.

[85] Tappert, p. 297.26.

[86] Jacobs, p. 83.

[87] Hunter, p. 177.

[88] Graham, p. 33.

[89] Augustine, p. 195.

[90] Fruchtenbaum, *Angelology* . . . , p. 8-9.

[91] Hunter, pp. 41, 170

[92] Graham, pp. 47-48.

[93] Davidson, pp. 336-337.

[94] *Ibid.*

[95] Fruchtenbaum, *Angelology* . . . , pp. 12-13.

[96] Graham, pp. 51-53.

[97] Fruchtenbaum, Angelology . . ., pp. 10-12.

[98] Ibid.

[99] Graham, pp. 50-51.

[100] Burnham, *A Book . . . , p. 92.*

[101] Fruchtenbaum, Angelology, . . . , p. 9.

[102] Graham, p. 43.

[103] Burnham, *A Book . . .* , p. 104

[104] Burnham, *A Book . . .* , p. 104.

[105] Fruchtenbaum, Angelology, . . . p. 9.

[106] Graham, p. 40.

[107] Burnham, *A Book . . .* , pp. 103-104.

[108] Hunter, p. 169.

[109] Fruchtenbaum, Angelology, . . . pp. 3-10.

[110] Burnham, *A Book . . .* , pp. 103-104.

[111] Augustine, pp. 141,240.

[112] Graham, pp. 39,45.

[113] Burnham, *An Angel . . .* , pp. 60-61.

[114] Fruchtenbaum, Angelology, . . . pp. 3-10.

[115] Hunter, p. 169.

[116] Graham, p. 40.

[117] Fruchtenbaum, Angelology, . . . p. 9.

[118] Graham, pp. 74, 99.

[119] Hunter, p. 195.

[120] Fruchtenbaum, *Angelology* . . . , pp. 14-15.

[121] Graham, p. 41.

[122] Fruchtenbaum, Satanology . . . , pp. 1, 7-10.

[123] Ibid.

[124] *Ibid.*

[125] Eade, chart 1

[126] Fruchtenbaum, Angelology . . . , p. 13

127 Eade, chart 1.

128 Graham, pp. 48, 55.

129 Fruchtenbaum, *Satanology* . . . , pp. 1-2. 10-11.

130 *Ibid.*

131 Plass, p. 402 (#1185, #1186).

132 Pittman, p. 11.

133 Fruchtenbaum, Satanology . . . , p. 10.

134 Christenson, p. 32.

135 Plass, p. 396 (#1165).

136 Fruchtenbaum, Satanology . . . , pp. 5-6.

137 Christensen, p. 32.

138 Augustine, pp. 225, 300.

139 Eade, chart 1.

140 Graham, p. 55.

141 Augustine, pp. 222, 306.

142 Fruchtenbaum, Satanology . . . , pp. 3-5.

143 Eade, chart 1.

144 Graham, pp. 56-57.

145 Fruchtenbaum, *Satanology* . . . , pp. 11-15

146 *Ibid.*

147 *Ibid.*

148 Plass, pp. 393, 393 (#1155 #1173).

149 Christenson, pp. 29-30

150 Augustine, pp. 306-311.

151 Plass, p. 393 (#1153).

152 Fruchtenbaum, Satanology . . . , p. 15.

153 Graham, pp. 57-59.

154 Christenson, p. 32.

155 Plass, p. 396 (#1165).

156 Fruchtenbaum, Satanology . . . , pp. 5-6.

157 Plass, p. 395 (#1163).

158 Eade, chart 2, part I.

159 Fruchtenbaum, Demonology . . . pp. 18-19.

160 Plass, pp. 394, 395, 401, 402(#1156, #1161, #1183, #1184).

161 Fruchtenbaum, Satanology . . . , pp. 20-21.

162 Plass, pp. 392, 394, 397 (#1150, #1152, #1156, #1168)

163 Hunter, p 167.

164 Pittman, pp. 8-9.

165 Augustine, p. 449.

166 Plass, pp. 395-397 (#1158, #1159, #1160, #1166, #1167).

167 Christenson, pp. 26-27.

168 Fruchtenbaum, *Demonology* . . . pp. 19-21.

169 Christenson, pp. 62-63.

170 *Ibid.*, pp. 19-20.

171 Fruchtenbaum, Demonology . . . pp. 1-4

[172] *Ibid.*
[173] Plass, p. 391,(#1149).
[174] Fruchtenbaum, *Demonology . . .* p. 12.
[175] Augustine, pp. 219-222. 244-246, 294.
[176] Pittman, pp. 11-12, 14, 18-20.
[177] Lewis, p. x.
[178] Fruchtenbaum, Demonology . . . pp. 9-11.
[179] Pittman, pp. 10-13.
[180] Eade, chart 1.
[181] Plass, pp., p. 393 (#1154).
[182] Pittman, pp. 55=56
[183] Pittman, p. 5.
[184] Fruchtenbaum, Demonology . . . p. 13.
[185] Augustine, p. 418.
[186] Fruchtenbaum, Demonology . . . pp. 19-26.
[187] Augustine, p. 321.
[188] Plass, pp., p. 393 (#1154).
[189] Fruchtenbaum, Satanology . . . , pp. 21-22.
[190] Hunter, p. 167.
[191] Graham, p. 36.
[192] Orr, pp. 133-134.
[193] Henry, Vol, p. 97
[194] Hunter, pp. 183-185.

ABOUT THE AUTHOR

Mark Erickson has been an adult Bible teacher for over 25 years. More than a teacher, he is a student of God's word. He has a military background, as well as an aviation background. He also has a Bachelor of Arts degree in political science, and a Masters of Science degree in counseling. All of these come together to present a very unique style that makes the topic very easy to comprehend.

CPSIA information can be obtained at www.ICGtesting.com
Printed in the USA
LVOW11s1545101114

412895LV00002B/443/A